Moms encouraging moms to know the love of Christ

The Wise Woman Enjoys

The Wise Woman Enjoys 2ⁿᵈ Edition

This book takes you from June — August

Designed by Kristall Willis   www.kwdesignsco.com

Copyright © 2019 Help Club For Moms

The Wise Woman Enjoys

Dearest Friend,

Welcome to *The Wise Woman Enjoys*, a devotional workbook based on God's Word, written for moms who long to enjoy their children during the long summer months and who desire to become messengers of joy in their homes. We are thankful you joined our band of sisters as we journey together in God's Word and seek to have our best, most joy-filled summer ever!

This book contains four Bible studies per week, spanning nine weeks. Each week is based on our summer theme: **The Summer of Joy!** We pray that this Summer of Joy encourages you to enjoy spending time with your children, re-focus your mind to operate joyfully, and ultimately embrace the Lord's call to motherhood. This calling is for every mother, whether you work a job to help support your family or stay at home full-time with your kids.

Are you ready to begin? Great, so are we! Through this study, we want to challenge you to commit <u>20 Minutes a Day to a Christ-Centered Home</u>.

Here's how:

- **Five Minutes of Prayer:** Start your time with the Lord by seeking Him in prayer! Praise Him for who He is and ask Him to reveal ways in which you can grow closer to Him through your time in His Word and this study. We also encourage you to find a prayer partner to pray with over the phone for ten minutes each week. Praying with another godly woman will change your life!

- **Ten Minutes in God's Word and Your *Wise Woman Enjoys* Study:** Read your study, being sure to refer to all Scriptures mentioned. There are only four studies each week, so feel free to spread each one out over two days, or dig deeper into the Scriptures mentioned on days that you do not have a study. We want spending time with the Lord to be doable for even the busiest mama! Make sure to use the journaling lines to jot down what God has taught you through your time with Him today! Make note of Scriptures or thoughts that stood out to you or write down how you plan to implement the "What's Next" ideas mentioned in each study.

- **Five Minutes to Prepare for Your Day:** Before you get up and hit the ground running, take five minutes to plan how you will be intentional about your day. Write down your "Six Most Important List" which is simply six things you desire to accomplish that day in your home. This list can include many things: perhaps a Mom Tip you would like to do (be sure to refer to the Mom Tips section each week!), a way you hope to encourage your husband or child that day, the meals you plan to prepare, or a task that needs to be finished in your home. Being intentional will make all the difference in both your impact on your family and the wellbeing of your home!

This workbook is designed to help you grow into the woman, wife, and mother you were created to be! As you walk through this study, we pray you will engage yourself in God's Word and open your heart to Him in prayer. Your life will be forever changed by making a habit of spending time with your Savior!

We pray for you to encounter Jesus and grow in spiritual wisdom and understanding as you actively participate in our study—*The Wise Woman Enjoys*.

Blessings and love,
The Help Club for Moms Team

P.S. – We would love to bless you for buying this book by gifting several exclusive FREE printables to you! Thank you for supporting the Help Club for Moms; we are so very blessed by you! **Check out myhelpclubformoms.com to access these printables.**

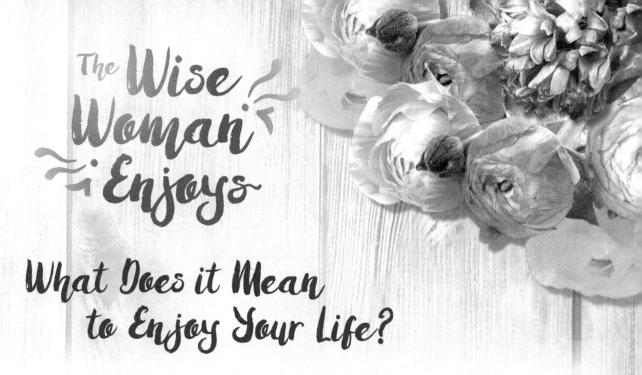

The Wise Woman Enjoys

What Does it Mean to Enjoy Your Life?

"Here is what I have seen to be good and fitting: to eat, to drink and enjoy oneself in all one's labor in which he toils under the sun during the few years of his life which God has given him; for this is his reward."

~ Ecclesiastes 5:18-20 (NASB)

For a lot of people, enjoying life is not complicated, but very simple. For moms, it's almost always complicated! I once heard someone say that motherhood is like going on a roller coaster ride every day, except each day is unique with a different roller coaster to ride! Wrapped up in twenty-four hours are high highs and low lows. Not just one high and one low, but *so many* of them that we can often feel exhausted and frazzled as we lay our head down at the end of the day.

I would even go so far as to say that most of us are merely surviving each day with a side of enjoying. We notice the sweet things our kids say that melt our hearts, the adorable look on their faces as they discover something new, or when they do that chore with gladness instead of grumbles (all the highs!). But usually, most of our days are overrun with laundry piles, temper tantrums, disobedience, making meals, doing dishes, homework battles, and the list goes on (the lows)...

Here is the thing, the God of the universe has said that it is important to *enjoy our lives!* Somewhere in the midst of our roller coaster, we are to experience the joy of it all. We should find satisfaction in the work we do, though it may seem mundane, and feel God's pleasure toward us as we take care of our families. When we feel God's pleasure, our heart's natural response is joy!

As we enter this beautiful summer season, take it all in, mama! Linger with your toddler for a few more seconds after he is calmed from a tantrum, bake cookies for that unruly teenager who just needs a little more love, and make dinner with joy in your heart knowing that the work of your hands is pleasing to God! There is fulfillment and joy even in the midst of the struggles and hidden places of motherhood. No matter the trench you find yourself in, God wants to gently pull you out and bring you into His light!

Join us as we give this summer to God and learn to *enjoy our lives!* We are blessed to have you journey along with us, and we pray that you find true encouragement through God's Holy Spirit on each and every page! We are praying for you!

Sincerely,
Krystle Porter and the Help Club for Moms Team

Culitvate Joy with the Word of God

As we begin to ponder what it means to grow and flourish as a Christ-follower, and learn how to live a joy-filled life, I can't think of a more beautiful picture than the one in Psalm 1:1-3:

> Blessed is the one who does not walk in step with the wicked or stand in the way that sinners take or sit in the company of mockers, but whose delight is in the law of the Lord, and who meditates on his law day and night. That person is like a tree planted by streams of water, which yields its fruit in season and whose leaf does not wither—whatever they do prospers.

Did you see what the Scripture says will happen to us when we meditate on the Word of God, day and night? It says that we will be like a tree planted by streams of water, which yields fruit and doesn't wither, and that we will also prosper in whatever we do. I don't know about you, but I deeply desire to prosper in all areas of my life, especially in the areas of my marriage and family relationships. We need to understand the love and words of Jesus. He has lots to say about how He wants us to live our lives, but we must plan and make space for the time it takes to spend each day pondering, praying, and listening.

May I invite you to commit yourself to the faithful study of the Word of God through this book? By committing yourself to do each of the Bible studies, you will rapidly find yourself growing into the Christian woman, wife, and mother you were created to be. Since there are only four short studies per week, this leaves other days where you can go back through the studies and read the whole chapter where the key verse is found. Remember to record what the Holy Spirit says to you in the journal pages provided. As always, before you begin each study, pray and ask Jesus to speak to you and help you to grow in Him and His love like never before.

Dearest sister, drink deep the words of our Lord, and the love and grace He offers you on a daily basis. When we draw our life from time spent with Jesus and fill ourselves up with His words of love, we find ourselves better equipped to do all that He has called us to do.

Remember, the words of Jesus when He said, "But whoever drinks the water I give him will never thirst. Indeed, the water I give him will become in him a fount of water springing up to eternal life" (John 4:14). When we feed on Jesus, we will never be hungry or thirsty again. Let Jesus fill you as you do this study. His Living Water will help you to flourish and prosper like never before!

We are praying for you!

Love,
Deb Weakly and the Help Club for Moms Team

Table of Contents

Table of Contents

The Wise Woman Enjoys

Summer of Joy

~ Week One ~

"Show me, Lord, my life's end and the number of my days; let me know how fleeting my life is."
– Psalm 39:4

Dear friends, welcome to Summer with the Help Club!

Ah, summer! I spend most of the year longing for summertime. It is by far my favorite time of year. If motherhood were a season, I think it would be summer. Just like the flowers blooming around us, we are growing and establishing ourselves. As we continue to grow and mature ourselves, we are charged with nurturing the new life that comes from us.

While I know this season will pass too quickly, I also know there will come a hot July day when there is work to do in the sun and no cloud or breeze in sight. Then I will wish for the peaceful cool of fall; I suspect I'm not the only one. I pray God will grant us wisdom to see how precious and fleeting this season is, that He will bless us with the respite we need to have joy as well as persistence through the dog days of summer.

I pray that each one of you will grow in your faith while doing these studies, praying, and living them out. I pray you will cherish your families and make many wonderful memories this summer!

Wishing you many blessings this week and throughout the summer!

With love,

Heather Doolittle and the Help Club For Moms Team

P.S. – Don't forget to print your **free, exclusive printables** available to you at **myhelpclubformoms.com**!

> **❝** *There are souls in this world which have the gift of finding joy everywhere and of leaving it behind them when they go.* **❞**
> *~ Frederick Faber*

Mom Tips

By: Leslie Leonard

The Mom Tips are designed to help you to grow closer to Jesus,
offer new ideas to help you to grow in your relationships with your husband
and children, and establish a Christ-centered home. At the beginning of each week,
simply pray about which tips to try and check them off as you accomplish them.
Completing them all or doing only one tip is just fine! As we say in the Help Club, *you do you!!*

The Wise Woman Builds Her Spirit

Memorize or place the following quote in an obvious place: *"When joy is a habit, loving
people is a reflex"* by Bob Goff. Practice joy with your people this week. Also, download a
voice recording app on your phone. If you do not have a smartphone, buy an inexpensive
voice recording device, and use this app or device to replay quotes and Scriptures you're
working on memorizing each week.

The Wise Woman Loves Her Husband

Pray for your husband today. Thank God for him and his influence in your life. Ask God to
fill him with the Holy Spirit to guide him through his day. You can even ask your husband
how you can be praying for him this week. Then write his prayer requests in your journal
or phone, and purpose to pray for him as much as you can. Set reminders on your phone so
you won't forget!

The Wise Woman Loves Her Children

Pack a picnic for your children and head to a local park or open space. Take time with your
children to appreciate the beauty of the world God created; stay and play too.

The Wise Woman Cares For Her Home

Create a specific space for all your children's outdoor toys and equipment in your garage or
backyard. This will make cleanup easier, and your children will always know where to look
for their items.

"You have captured my heart, my treasure, my bride.
You hold it hostage with one glance of your eyes,
with a single jewel of your necklace. Your love delights me,
my treasure, my bride. Your love is better than wine,
your perfume more fragrant than spices."

~ Song of Solomon 4:9-10 (NLT)

Dating Your Husband Matters!

By: Rachel Jones

Summer is such a sweet season. The sun warms our bodies, the flowers make us smile...And is there anything better than watching our kids play gleefully at a park? Another wonderful thing that summer brings is the late sunsets and gentle nights, which are perfect for going on dates with our husbands. I have been married for 16 years, and I am still not an expert on dating my husband. Over the years, we have appreciated the times when a date would land in our laps, such as when grandparents were visiting, but we have struggled to make consistent dating a priority.

About six months ago, my husband and I both decided that our marriage needed to come first, and no matter what our schedule brought, we would have weekly date nights. With four children, we knew this would be difficult, but we challenged each other to take this new commitment seriously. We wanted to laugh more, create new memories, and grow our desire for each other. Today's verse is a powerful reminder of what most of us had in the early years of marriage, but those thoughts and feelings take work after being together for a while. Deep down in our hearts, my husband and I both knew that we wanted our marriage to become exciting and romantic again and that it was worth the investment in time and money.

Over the years, I had wondered why going out on dates with my husband truly mattered. We regularly made time for each other at night, we were affectionate with each other and hardly ever fought. But we still knew there was more. God didn't just create marriage to be a pleasant relationship that produces children. He created the union of marriage to forge two sinners together to sharpen, love, support, respect, and challenge the other, for a lifetime. This love is a serious commitment and takes great faith. I love the way Psalms 85:10 (AMP) uses the term "steadfast love,"— "Steadfast love and truth and faithfulness meet together; righteousness and peace kiss each other."

Peace. That word describes just one of the results from intentional date nights with your spouse. As busy parents, it is hard to find time to truly connect. Date nights allow for unhurried conversation, which every marriage needs to grow. My husband and I have also appreciated that our date nights give us the chance to talk about things besides our kids and logistics. Mamas, aren't you with me when I say that it is so special to just look into our husband's eyes, and have him smile at us? My hope for you all this summer are many, many nights spent enjoying time with your husband.

Going Deeper:

If you don't have a trustworthy and reliable babysitter, pray about it. God will send you someone your children will love if that is what your hearts truly desires.

If money is a hindrance, pray for another couple friend you trust, and ask them if they would like to "trade" date nights with you. You watch their kids and then they watch yours. You and your husband get a weekly date without paying for a sitter and your children get a playdate. Win, win!

Week One ~ Day One

What's Next:

All too often on date night, my husband and I fall into the habit of talking about our children and/or scheduling issues. To counteract this routine, we have really enjoyed using these thoughtful questions. Take them with you the next time you and your hubby go out!

1. What is your favorite Bible verse and why?
2. If money were not an option, what job would you have? Also, where would you want to live?
3. What was your proudest moment?
4. When you get to heaven, what one question do you want to ask God?
5. What is the sweetest thing I ever did for you?

Another aspect of date night that can get stale is what you and your husband actually do. Going out to eat at a restaurant is always nice, but here are some other fun ideas!

6. Go on a hike and bring along a picnic.
7. Visit a few model homes together and daydream/discuss ideas for your own home...or future home.
8. Go to three different restaurants! One for appetizers, another for dinner, and then another (or bakery) for dessert. This idea is also a lot of fun if you can park near all the restaurants and then walk from place to place. A cute downtown adds to the festivity!
9. Attend a concert, musical, TED talk, art gallery opening, or science exhibit together. Discuss this part of culture and why you like or dislike it.
10. Go to Barnes and Noble and browse books together. Sit in the cafe and have a coffee or scone. Bring a pack of cards or the questions from above and just relax. Most Barnes and Nobles are open until 10:00 on the weekends!

Journal

_____

_____

_____

_____

_____

_____

_____

_____

_____

_____

_____

"Always be humble and gentle. Be patient with each other, making allowance for each other's faults because of your love. Make every effort to keep yourselves united in the Spirit, binding yourselves together with peace."

~ Ephesians 4:2-3 (NLT)

A Peaceful Home

By: Mari Jo Mast

Since summer is here and school is out, your children have more free time. So I'm wondering if you're dealing with more sibling rivalry and behavior issues? This happens in my home.

As a younger mom, I often expected a great deal of perfection from my kids. I regret it now because I realize my unrealistic standards and high ideals kept me from loving them well. It actually caused more strife.

Sometimes, when we think our children need more rules, they really need to be shown the way. How we parent plays a big role; we can either lead them to or away from Jesus. He alone can change a child's sinful heart, and more rules can never do that. Although we must set guidelines, they should only serve and exist because of the greater law of love. In our own lives, we know God's loving kindness helps us repent and live better. We can pass this on to our children.

Moms, don't sweat the small stuff! When we become overwhelmed and desperate, we tend to do crazy things we regret later. When a "strife" moment happens, we can choose the high road (1 Corinthians 13). How we as moms handle strife can either heighten it or help diminish it. We can't eradicate it from our lives completely, but God can show us how to usher in an atmosphere of peace instead of more conflict.

Please know this season of motherhood is short! Now my children are older, and I know this is true. A glimmer of light beams at the end of the tunnel, and it brightens with time. Before you know it, your little babies will be all grown-up, and your nest will be empty! Give yourself permission to enjoy them while you still can. Live with no regrets. Don't beat yourself up when you make a mistake; remember, it's never too late to start over.

Below, I've listed a few practical steps from God's Word to help you navigate through times of strife. Though God's ways don't always make sense to our natural mind, without a doubt, we can trust His Word. His wisdom supersedes our own by a long stretch!

Above all, remember God's faithfulness covers even your worst failures!

Six Steps to Enjoy a More Peaceful Home:

1. **Relax:** Make an allowance for your kid's faults (Ephesians 4:2). They are going to mess up, and it's okay. Jesus already knows, and that's why He came! Lead them to the One who empowers them to overcome sin.

2. **Walk in humility:** Don't parent out of pride. If your kids misbehave in public or act up around your friend's kids, smile and simply say, "So sorry, we're trying to work on this right now." Admit it when your kids are wrong but don't shame them.

3. **Respond gently:** Proverbs 15:1 (NKJV) says, "A soft answer turns away wrath, but harsh words stir up anger." Whoa...this is a tough one, but it totally works! Breathe a prayer as you count to ten if you're angry.

4. **Have patience:** James 1:19b (NLT) says, "You must all be quick to listen, slow to speak, and slow to get angry." Best advice ever!

5. **Let Jesus lead you:** Galatians 5:17-18 says, "But if you are led by the Spirit, you are not under the Law." Wow, think about that one! Ask God what He thinks, carefully listen, and then obey. The Spirit gives life, but the law strengthens sin. Ask God to fill you with His Spirit.

6. **Live in peace:** As you apply the first five steps above, the peace of Jesus will reign in your home (Ephesians 4:3b).

Go Deeper:

Our precious children are beautiful gifts from God's hand. Reflect on your parenting. Does it bring peace or more strife? Ask for God's heart on parenting.

Hug and kiss your kids often. Tell them you're sorry if you've been short or angry with them lately.

What's Next?

Pray with me: *"Jesus, you lead so well. I cannot thank you enough for always caring, loving, and forgiving me when I mess up. You allow me to fail. You are so humble and aren't offended at all when I disobey you. I can hardly believe how patient and gentle you are with me! I want you to help me parent my kids because your ways always work and lead to peace! Amen."*

journal

_____

_____

_____

_____

_____

_____

_____

_____

_____

_____

_____

_____

"Love the Lord your God with all your heart and with all your soul and with all your strength. These commandments that I give you today are to be on your hearts. Impress them on your children. Talk about them when you sit at home and when you walk along the road, when you lie down and when you get up."

~ Deuteronomy 6:5-7

Give Your Children the Gift of God's Word

By: Tara Davis & Deb Weakly

Mamas, we have such an important task before us in impressing God's Word on the hearts of our precious children. Praise the Lord that we are not alone! He is here to guide us, and He graciously gives us practical instruction in the Bible on how to lovingly inspire our children to follow Him.

First, God tells us that His commandments are to be on our hearts (Deuteronomy 6:6). We must spend time daily in the Bible ourselves! We are not able to impart something to our children that we do not know. We must know God's words as intimately as we know our own thoughts (Joshua 1:8-9). Through our intimacy with His Word, we can speak wisdom to our children in a manner that will personally reach their hearts as they have questions about God and His ways.

Secondly, God tells us that we are to talk about His Word when we "sit at home and walk along the road, when [we] lie down and when [we] get up" (Deuteronomy 6:7). Discussing things of the Lord, praising Him, and seeking Him are to be daily rhythms in our homes. This rhythm must first start with reading God's Word to our children. Sweet friend, do not neglect this step because your children are too young, you find the Bible confusing, or your family is busy. God will provide the time and understanding you need (James 4:8). All you have to do is ask!

From there, use your creativity! Notice and thank God with your children for His small blessings. Sing songs together to memorize the books of the Bible or Scripture. Pray with your children for the hurts, cares, and celebrations in their daily lives (1 Thessalonians 5:16-18). Talk to them about their thoughts on passages or stories you have read. Be intentional each day about sharing God in a way that connects with the hearts of your children. You are building their foundation for a dynamic, lifetime relationship with Him (Proverbs 22:6).

Go Deeper:

As your children grow and begin to read God's Word on their own, it is very important for them to understand the layout of the Bible. It is a huge book and can be overwhelming. Memorizing the books of the Bible together can be so helpful in preparing them, and what better way to do this than through music!

Pick up a copy of the *Wee Sing Bible Songs* CD or purchase just the "Old Testament" and "New Testament" songs on iTunes. These two catchy songs are a fantastic way to commit to memory the books of the Bible and will remain with your children for a lifetime!

You can also take it one step further and play a fun game with your children. Simply write all the books of either the Old or New Testament on index cards. As the song plays, take turns laying out the cards on the floor in the correct order. Challenge yourselves to keep up with the music!

What's Next?

If you are anything like me, you like to see what has worked for other mamas! Here is a list of Help Club recommendations to encourage you on this path of sharing Christ daily with your sweet children.

- *Wee Sing Bible Songs*
- *The Action Bible* by Doug Mauss (great for children who like comic books)
- *The Jesus Storybook Bible* by Sally Lloyd Jones (great for birth – 6-year-olds)
- *Child's Story Bible* by Catherine Vos (great for 4 – 12-year-olds)
- *Seeds Family Worship* CD's (fantastic Scripture memory)

Journal

_____

_____

_____

_____

_____

_____

_____

_____

_____

_____

_____

_____

_____

_____

_____

_____

_____

_____

_____

"Now may the Lord of peace himself give you peace
at all times and in every way. The Lord be with all of you."

~ 2 Thessalonians 3:16

Begin With the End in Mind

By: Heather Doolittle

If you're like me, your Summer begins with enthusiastic joy—no more soccer practices during dinnertime, end-of-the-year party preparations, or frantic searches for winter coats and boots! Yet somehow that enthusiasm turns to a feeling of drudgery as your children's squabbling escalates and summer drags on. Instead of succumbing to this pattern, begin this season with the end in mind—not just the end of summer, but the end-result of your parenting.

"The best way to predict your future is to create it." – Abraham Lincoln

What is it that you want from this Summer? Set realistic personal or family goals. Keep them as your primary focus this season, and give yourself extra grace in other areas.

It is better to improve one area of your life permanently than make 1,000 ambitious, unsustainable changes that will fall by the wayside within a few weeks.

Make sure you know what you are going to change, how you are going to change it, and why it is your priority and support it with Scripture. Having a goal that is rooted in Scripture will help you stick to it; it will remain a high priority when your to-do list is a mile long.

Here are some examples of summer goals that I have set over the years:

What	Why	How	Scripture
Spend more quality time as a family.	Your weekends will be restful, and your home will be more peaceful the next week.	Prepare for a great weekend by making treats, assembling crockpot meals, and cleaning the house on Fridays.	John 14:27 2 Thessalonians 3:16
Teach your children to go through their morning routines without your help.	Kids take pride in caring for themselves, and it feels positively indulgent to start the day with a hot cup of tea and some quiet time.	Let even small children dress themselves and retrieve food prepared the night before. It takes time and consistency to begin a routine and form a habit.	Proverbs 22:6 Isaiah 54:13
Incorporate your faith and the Bible into your family's daily rhythms.	It takes time and intentionality to disciple children and teach them to relate to Jesus personally. Don't just assume your faith is rubbing off on your children.	Take note of how God is woven into your daily life, and consider adding more of Him. Pray about how to demonstrate and explain your relationship with Jesus for your children.	Deuteronomy 11:18-20 2 Timothy 3:16-17

Remember to give plenty of grace to yourself and your children. The goal is to keep realistic expectations so that you can enjoy one another's company! With just a few months of focused effort, you will reap the benefits for years.

Go Deeper:

How can you use this summer to grow closer to God or your family?

Pray about it, and then don't stress. Give that area over to God. Put forth an honest effort and trust that God will work with what you have to offer.

What's Next?

Prayerfully consider coming up with your own goals for the summer (or any other time of year). Just make sure you have a *how* and *why* and find Scripture to support it. Looking to Scripture for support will ensure that you are choosing a worthwhile goal (getting your body swimsuit-ready is fine, but unless you're planning on becoming a swimsuit model, you probably shouldn't make it your *primary* focus *all summer long*).

Remember to choose one reasonable and important goal, and don't stress about it. I am working on the third row of the table above. The other two are from summers past.

Scripture References

Thessalonians 3:16 "Now may the Lord of peace himself give you peace at all times in every way. The Lord be with you all."

Proverbs 22:6 "Start children off on the way they should go, and even when they are old they will not turn from it."

Deuteronomy 11:18-20 "Fix these words of mine in your hearts and minds; tie them as symbols on your hands and bind them on your foreheads. Teach them to your children, talking about them when you sit at home and when you walk along the road, when you lie down and when you get up. Write them on the doorframes of your houses and on your gates."

Journal

_____

_____

_____

_____

_____

_____

_____

_____

_____

Best Scripture Memory Contest Ever!

By: Tara Davis

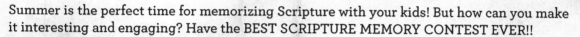

"I have hidden your word in my heart that I might not sin against you."
– Psalm 119:11

Summer is the perfect time for memorizing Scripture with your kids! But how can you make it interesting and engaging? Have the BEST SCRIPTURE MEMORY CONTEST EVER!!

These short verses make it super easy! Just choose a simple reward system for your kids...perhaps a treasure box with tiny treats or dollar store prizes, a special day out after completing a number of verses, or maybe a family movie night for meeting a verse goal. It can be super simple! Cut these verses into strips, place them in a jar and let your children choose a verse to begin. They can make their Scripture into a song, come up with hand-motions for it, do a physical activity such as jumping jacks or hopscotch while reciting the words, or write the verse out and illustrate it.

There are so many ways to make Scripture memory fun! Plus, knowing Scripture fills our kids' little hearts with wisdom and helps them to enjoy life! See how many short verses your kids can memorize this summer!

1. Acts 16:31 – Believe on the Lord Jesus Christ and you will be saved.
2. Philippians 4:4 – Rejoice in the Lord always.
3. Psalm 145:9 – The Lord is good to all.
4. Romans 5:8 – While we were still sinners, Christ died for us.
5. Romans 3:23 – All people have sinned and fall short of the glory of God.
6. Proverbs 3:5 – Trust in the Lord with all your heart.
7. 1 John 5:3 – This is love for God: to obey His commands.
8. Ephesians 6:1 – Children, obey your parents in the Lord, for this is right.
9. Psalm 136:1 – Give thanks to the Lord, for He is good. His love endures forever.
10. Philippians 4:13 – I can do everything through Him who gives me strength.
11. Luke 6:31 – Do to others as you would have them do to you.
12. Deuteronomy 6:5 – You shall love the Lord your God with all your heart and with all your soul and with all your might.
13. Matthew 28:6 – He is not here, He has risen!
14. John 4:19 – We love because He first loved us.
15. Ephesians 4:32 – Be kind to one another.
16. Psalm 150:6 – Let everything that has breath praise the Lord.
17. Psalm 56:3 – When I am afraid, I will trust in you.
18. Psalm 139:14 – I praise you God, for I am fearfully and wonderfully made.
19. 1 Thessalonians 5:17 – Pray without ceasing.
20. Colossians 3:2 – Set your minds on things above, not on earthly things.

Summer of Joy

~ Week Two ~

Dear Sweet Mamas!

How is your summer going? I pray your time with your kids at home is fun! It will be over before you know it!

The phrase, "The days are long but the years are short" is *so* true! I *really* miss the days when my children were in my home.

Even though many of the days felt stressful and tiring, I would still start over from day one. I can honestly say that asking God to help me to "savor the days" with my kids really made a difference in my attitude and my heart.

When we pray verses such as Psalm 39:4, "Show me, LORD, my life's end and the number of my days; let me know how fleeting my life is," it helps us to enjoy the days with our family instead of taking them for granted.

My challenge for you this week is to write this verse on a little card and keep it at your kitchen sink. Make them your life's prayer for this season with your kids at home.

It's going to be a great summer! We are praying for you!

With love,

Deb Weakly and the Help Club For Moms Team

> *Joy is the serious business of Heaven.*
> ~ C.S. Lewis

Mom Tips

By: Leslie Leonard

The Mom Tips are designed to help you to grow closer to Jesus,
offer new ideas to help you to grow in your relationships with your husband
and children, and establish a Christ-centered home. At the beginning of each week,
simply pray about which tips to try and check them off as you accomplish them.
Completing them all or doing only one tip is just fine! As we say in the Help Club, *you do you!!*

The Wise Woman Builds Her Spirit

Start each day this week with a grateful heart. Write down in your journal five things for which you feel grateful every day. Also, get a pad of spiral bound index cards and write Psalm 119:105 on it. Keep it at your kitchen sink this week so that you can see it often and commit it to memory.

The Wise Woman Loves Her Husband

Choose a book to read together as a couple. Set aside a specific time together to discuss what you are learning and experiencing from your reading. Some great suggestions are *The Heavenly Man* by Brother Yun, *The 4:8 Principle: The Secret to a Joy-Filled Life* by Tommy Newberry, and *Crazy Love* by Francis Chan and Danae Yankoski.

The Wise Woman Loves Her Children

Have a S'mores night with your children to teach them Scripture! Gather up the graham crackers, chocolate, and marshmallows and head outside. Use your backyard fire pit or grill to roast the marshmallows. While eating your yummy treat, teach your children Hebrews 12:28-29: "...God is a consuming fire." God's fire completely transforms us, just as fire transforms marshmallows and chocolate into delicious goodness!

The Wise Woman Cares For Her Home

Focus on setting a beautiful table, complete with candles and centerpieces. Decor and music can make a regular weeknight dinner fun!

"I have fought the good fight, I have finished the course,
I have kept the faith; in the future there is laid up for me the
crown of righteousness, which the Lord, the righteous Judge,
will award to me on that day; and not only to me,
but also to all who have loved His appearing."
~ 2 Timothy 4:7-8 (NASB)

5 Spiritual Anchors For Moms

By: Mari Jo Mast

"Motherhood takes...the strength of Samson, the wisdom of Solomon, the patience of Job, the faith of Abraham, the insight of Daniel and the courage of David!" – Unknown

Do you ever wonder if you can weather the storms of motherhood and still be okay when you come out on the other end? Me too!

I have seven children who are older now, and my youngest has reached the age of almost 8 years. Baby-land and toddler-hood are a thing of the past, yet I believe my job as mother will continue until I take my last breath. As I look back on the "hurricane season" (what I call early motherhood) and enjoy my life presently while I fix my eyes on what lies ahead, there are a few Scriptures I recognize that have helped and still help keep me grounded. I want to share them with you. I cling to these foundational Scriptures with all that I am because my calling and well-being depend on it. I cannot imagine life without them.

With God's help, we can fight the good fight of mom-hood, and we can win!

As you read and meditate on the truths from God's Word (below), I pray they bring joy and hope to your spirit, soul, and body. We can find everything we will ever need as moms somewhere in God's Word. Take hope and heart!

1. **The Holy Spirit is my teacher.** Have you asked the Holy Spirit to come into your inner-most being, to fill you? We *need* the Spirit of Jesus to teach us how to mother our children, to raise them in righteousness. The impossibility of the job begs us to cry out! It would be cruel for God not to provide a teacher for us when we need one, which is basically 24/7. Our answer lies in Him. John 14:26 (NKJV) reads: "But the Helper, the Holy Spirit, whom the Father will send in My name, He will teach you all things..."

    Listen! Nothing too small or too large in our mom world takes God by surprise—not the kids fighting and arguing until we can't stand it anymore, the baby fussing relentlessly, us getting no sleep at night, or our teenager being stuck in a sticky dating relationship. He already knows everything.

    Catch this: the most up-to-date and relevant teaching we will ever find lies at our fingertips. God *wants* to fill and help instruct us, and He exceeds state-of-the-art standards to beat. He teaches any willing heart freely! Just ask.

2. **I can do all things.** Notice I didn't say "God can do all things." Although this is true, God fully equips and gives us the power to overcome any obstacle we face through His Spirit. This stands true for every mom who has asked the Holy Spirit to dwell inside of her. I never, ever thought it possible to be a mom of seven children, yet here I am. The Holy Spirit gives me strength. When Jesus comes to dwell in us, we become yoked with Him, and everything becomes possible!

Philippians 4:13 (NKJV) says, "I can do all things through Christ who strengthens me." This truth takes faith. Only believe!

3. **God sees me; He knows my name:** Every mom on this earth has a desire to be known, especially by God! The silent and difficult road of motherhood we climb daily with our children, though often filled with unspeakable joy, can threaten to undo us. We can find solace in the Gospel of John, chapter 10 verse 14: The sheep hear his voice, and he calls his own sheep by name...I am the good shepherd, and know my sheep. Mom, Jesus notices, appreciates, and understands every obstacle you face. Notice: He is the good Shepherd with a capital "S." Good Shepherds rescue vulnerable sheep in trouble, and Jesus does this perfectly and beautifully. How comforting that He sees and knows His own sheep by name, even you.

4. **This too shall pass.** With time as our friend, it goes slowly enough for us to prove to our children we love them, yet quickly enough to keep us on our toes! Ecclesiastes 3:1 (NASB) says, "There is an appointed time for everything. And there is a time for every event under heaven." Here's the mom-hood scope: In your very near future (believe me, sooner than you think), a time will come when your kids will no longer be solely dependent on you. They eventually reach adulthood. Glory Hallelujah! You will still have the name "mom," but your role will change to mentor and friend. There is a time for everything. In regard to the challenging role we sometimes have to fulfill right now, know "this too shall pass."

5. **I reap what I sow.** Galatians 6:7 (NLT) says, "Don't be misled—you cannot mock the justice of God. You will always harvest what you plant." I find this very convicting! Whatever I hand out to my children today, they willingly give back in return later. Kindness reaps kindness. Anger reaps anger. Love reaps love. Selfishness reaps selfishness. Joy reaps joy. I get to choose what I glean in the future. Value this truth of reaping. The more time we spend with Jesus, talking to Him, reading His Word, involving Him in our everyday lives, the more the Holy Spirit's fruit will pour out of us! We cannot produce good qualities unless we surrender everything to Him. We need to die daily, lay our lives down at His feet, and obey Him instead of our flesh. We most definitely reap what we sow.

Go Deeper:

Let Jesus take the position of "BFF" (Best Friend Forever) in your life. He finds and takes us to good places in motherhood. He never gives the wrong advice but gently leads those with young (Isaiah 40:11).

What's Next?

Memorize these five Scriptures. Write them on sticky notes and place them where you will frequently notice them, such as the kitchen sink, bathroom mirror, or in your car. Here are the Scriptures:

• John 14:26   • Philippians 4:13   • John 10:14   • Ecclesiastes 3:1   • Galatians 6:7

Look them up in your favorite translation and let them stabilize you, like pegs you can hold onto when life gets hard.

journal

_____

_____

_____

_____

"These words I am commanding you today are to be upon your hearts. And you shall teach them diligently to your children and speak of them when you sit in your house and when you walk along the road, when you lie down and when you get up. Tie them as reminders on your hands and bind them on your foreheads. Write them on the doorposts of your houses and on your gates."

~ Deuteronomy 6:6-9

Intentionality with the Television

By: Rachel Jones

Summertime and TV-watching go hand-in-hand. Kids are home all day, so the television can very quickly become the babysitter. After all, it surely keeps the children occupied and quiet so you can get a few things done! I totally understand that mamas, as I currently have four young children in my home. However, I think we all know this isn't best for them.

What if, instead, we created an environment in our homes where television watching could actually provide something positive? My heart wants to show you that with some intentionality, TV can become an excellent learning experience for your family. It can also become a special time to share something together, create memories, and cuddle on the couch.

Today's verse in Deuteronomy says to "teach them diligently." In my opinion, that can happen all day long if we take advantage of the openings our children give us. Proverbs 23:26 says, "my son, give me your heart and let your eyes delight in my ways." Our children are waiting to be instructed by us and here are some suggestions on how to use TV to make that happen:

1. **TV can be a great conversation starter.**
   "…Bring them up in the training and instruction of the Lord" (Ephesians 6:4b). Some topics are not easy to discuss with kids, particularly with pre-teens and teens. Bringing up hard subjects can often turn into awkward moments. However, by choosing programs that address sensitive topics and by following His instruction, you will have the open door to train your child in the instruction of the Lord.

2. **TV can be educational and fun!**
   In our home, we enjoy cuddling up together to watch a show where something new is being exposed or taught to our children. As the parents, we intentionally choose certain shows beforehand. We then watch together, laugh together, and discuss anything new we saw or learned. Watching quality television creates great memories!

3. **TV exposes our children to different cultures.**
   Many TV programs can be powerful tools in teaching our children about new cultures and their lifestyles and traditions. Documentaries or dramas filmed in other countries can also help our children feel empathy for those living in poverty, or develop curiosity about their traditions.

<u>Go Deeper:</u>

Pray about how you view television in your home. Ask the Lord to guide you towards shows that are edifying and in line with Christian teachings.

What's Next?

I am praying that all of you mamas have a great summer of TV watching with your children. Below is my list of shows/documentaries we have watched in our home that I would love to share with you. All of these are available to stream on Netflix or Amazon.

Pre-School/Kindergarten

1. Wild Kratts https://pbskids.org/wildkratts/
2. Creative Galaxy https://www.amazon.com/Creative-Galaxy-Season-101/dp/B00CB6VTDS
3. The Hive http://www.thehivetvshow.com/#home
4. Word Party https://www.netflix.com/title/80063705

Early Elementary

1. Odd Squad https://pbskids.org/oddsquad/
2. Bindi's Bootcamp https://www.australiazoo.com.au/bindis-bootcamp/
3. Zoo Clues https://tvproductioncompany.wixsite.com/eiprogamming/zooclues
4. Space Racers https://www.spaceracers.com/

Upper Elementary

1. Brain Games https://www.nationalgeographic.com/tv/brain-games/
2. Annedroids https://www.amazon.com/Annedroids-Season-1/dp/B00CB6FHKE
3. On the Way to School http://www.distribfilmsus.com/our-movies/on-the-way-to-school/
4. Blue Planet 2 https://www.bbcearth.com/blueplanet2/

Journal

_____

_____

_____

_____

_____

_____

_____

_____

_____

_____

_____

"I have hidden your Word in my heart that
I might not sin against you."
~ Psalm 119:11

Making the Bible Come Alive for Young Children

By: Tara Davis

We are instructed in Psalm 119:11 to keep God's words close to our heart, to intertwine them into the very fabric of our being so that they will intimately influence our lives. Until recently, I didn't realize how important that calling is for my children too! As parents, it is tempting to rely on Sunday school to encourage and instruct our children in the ways of the Lord. However, Deuteronomy 6:7 charges us as parents with teaching God's Word to our children!

How do we teach our children to love the Lord? How do we take ancient, sometimes conceptually abstract biblical stories and help our children see them as more than just fairytales? We must allow God's Word to deeply invade our hearts and homes so that experiencing its truths becomes as much a part of our day as breathing!

We can facilitate our children in forming personal connections with God's Word through engaging their minds and their senses. Let me share some fun, hands-on ideas you can try with your young children!

1. Encourage your children to act out the stories you read from the Bible. Provide simple costumes or props, but remember it doesn't have to be fancy to make an impression.

2. Provide your children with a special art notebook they can use to connect through illustration with stories you have read.

3. Encourage children to become "Bible reporters." Start a family newspaper in which they can write about biblical stories as if they are exciting current events.

4. Make daily devotions a sweet time! Psalm 119:103 tells us that God's words are like honey on our lips. Keep treats like small chocolates or lollipops on hand and indulge during your daily Bible-time together.

5. Encourage your children to include what you are reading in their play. Children connect with heroic stories or complex concepts in this way!

6. Memorize Scripture together. Make it fun with special rewards and exciting goals to work toward.

7. Weave lessons about God into routine events. Bath time may be a wonderful opportunity to share the story of Noah's flood with your young child. And the loneliness that an older child is feeling may allow him to truly connect with the loving presence and companionship that Jesus offers.

This is just a small sampling of ideas. Brainstorm to come up with ways to reach the heart and unique personality of your children for God's kingdom!

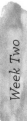
Go Deeper:
Mamas, the most important thing you can do to connect your child with the Bible is study it together regularly! Whether you use a devotional book, a children's Bible, or your own Bible, let it be a daily ritual to engage in God's Word together. Additionally, let your children see you studying God's Word and pursuing a passionate relationship with Him. They will model their behavior after yours!

What's Next?
Pray and ask God to meet the needs of your children's hearts. Ask God to make Himself known to your children in a way that only He can. His love for your children is deeper than anyone could ever imagine (Ephesians 3:17-19)!

journal

_____

_____

_____

_____

_____

_____

_____

_____

_____

_____

_____

_____

_____

_____

_____

_____

_____

"Finally, brothers and sisters, whatever is true, whatever is noble, whatever is right, whatever is pure, whatever is lovely, whatever is admirable—if anything is excellent or praiseworthy—think about such things."

~ Philippians 4:8

Making Memories through God's Creation

By: Krystle Porter

Summer monsoon storms have been coming and going through Phoenix the past couple of weeks. It has brought some much-needed reprieve from the oven-like, 110 degree temperatures! Tonight, I listened to the thunder roll while cooking dinner and serving it outside on our table. Then, I put an old record on our player, lit a couple of candles, and spread out a pretty tablecloth. I called my family when dinner was ready, and my kids "oohed" and "ahhed" at the dark, cloud-filled sky and the "fancy" table I had prepared for us. We had a beautiful night. My sweet 5-year-old ended our time saying she wished every night could be like this.

Let me give you a little background to the above scene. First, we had a bare fridge, so dinner was rice and beans! Next, my "fancy" tablecloth was actually an old curtain I had lying around, and the record I played was 99 cents from Goodwill! I always imagined I needed to have a lot of money and time to create a "fancy" experience for my family to enjoy. It didn't occur to me that it can happen in the smallest of ways. Tonight was simple and cheap, but no one minded what we were having or where it came from; it was all about the feeling and love it was coupled with! We do not need expensive things to create a beautiful memory for our family or children. We just need to be intentional and aware of the beauty God has already placed in front of us!

I love how Philippians 4:8 encourages us to focus on beauty and goodness. God has created beauty all around us through nature. Just like the verse in Philippians, I could not help but ponder and "ooh" and "ahh" over His lovely and praiseworthy creation tonight! God gives us so many opportunities to partner with Him in His creation. Choosing to partner with God tonight as I enjoyed His beauty with my family was a precious memory I hope not to forget.

The Bible says in Psalm 19:1: "The heavens declare the glory of God; the skies proclaim the work of his hands."

Psalm 147:8 (NKJV) says: "Who covers the heaven with clouds, who prepares rain for the earth, who makes grass to grow upon the mountains."

And Psalm 8:3-4 (ESV) says: "When I look at your heavens, the work of your fingers, the moon and the stars, which you have set in place, what is man that you are mindful of him, and the son of man that you care for him?"

Partnering with God and His creation helps to give us perspective; perspective on the majesty and goodness of God. He created this earth for us to enjoy and draw us to Him. And He wants us to share this with our children too!

Go Deeper:

Have you experienced God recently through His creation/nature? Write down one verse from this study and meditate on it this week! Then make time to be with God in some way (even a small way) in nature!

What's Next?

Invite the kids to join you! Tell them about God and His creation and love for them. Read them the verse you have meditated on. Ask them to point out some lovely things along the way that they enjoy about His creation. Make a memory!

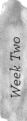

Journal

_____

_____

_____

_____

_____

_____

_____

_____

_____

_____

_____

_____

_____

_____

_____

_____

_____

_____

How many of you love to eat vegetables right from the garden? It is such a rewarding and truly tasty experience. Not many of us have the luxury of having a garden or benefiting from farm to table. Thankfully, we have local grocers or farm stands to purchase from. This Heirloom Tomato French Bread Pizza is ripe tomato and basil pesto at its finest. I love the splash of color from the tomatoes and find this is an excellent appetizer during the summer for just about any occasion!

HEIRLOOM TOMATO FRENCH BREAD PIZZA

By: Rae-Ellen Sanders

Ingredients

A loaf of French (or Italian) bread—sliced in half lengthwise

A container of heirloom grape tomatoes, sliced

Small jar of basil pesto sauce (6 ounces)

1 cup shredded Mozzarella cheese

¼ cup shaved Parmesan cheese

A drizzle of olive oil

1 tbsp. balsamic vinegar

Pinch red pepper flakes

Heirloom tomatoes make this fun French Bread Pizza a gourmet treat! The different shades pop with color and make this version a seasonal specialty. This is so easy to arrange, especially with prepared pesto. This is a perfect appetizer for any summer event.

Directions:

1. Cut your French/Italian bakery bread lengthwise and place on a baking sheet.
2. Spread prepared pesto on top.
3. Slice tomatoes in halves or in disc slices, as some tomatoes will vary in size.
4. Place sliced tomatoes in a bowl and add one tablespoon of balsamic vinegar and stir.
5. Spread tomato mixture evenly on top of the pesto.
6. Sprinkle a combination of both kinds of cheese on top.
7. Drizzle olive oil and then sprinkle red pepper flakes if desired.
8. Bake at 400 degrees for 10-12 minutes.

Summer of Joy

~ Week Three ~

"There is a time for everything, and a season for every activity under the heavens."
– Ecclesiastes 3:1

Hello Dear Mamas!

I trust you're having a lot of fun and enjoying this wonderful summer season with your beautiful children!

I always enjoy working outside, mowing the lawn, and planting and watering flowers with my children, as well as having a more flexible schedule when school is finally out. The weeks fly by, and I want to do all I can to make good memories. We have a membership at a local bowling alley for the next few months, and I can't wait to spend more time together competing even though I hardly ever win!

I pray you have the energy and strength it takes to keep up with your children the next few weeks. What sweet little blessings God has entrusted to us!

I wonder if you've created a summer to-do list and what that might include?

I'm trying to be more intentional right now. Here are a few things I'm working on:
  • Planning one or two fun family activities per week.
  • Hugging my children more often.
  • Including them more in my daily activities.
  • Being more aware of my words and taking the time to affirm my family members more often.

All of us on The Help Club team are rooting for you! We are praying for you to see the hearts of your children and for the wisdom of God to be imparted to you. We mothers have the most important job in the world.

With love,

Mari Jo Mast and the Help Club For Moms Team

"Find ecstasy in life; the mere sense of living is joy enough.
~ *Emily Dickinson*

Mom Tips

By: Leslie Leonard

The wise woman builds her house.
~ Proverbs 14:1a

The Wise Woman Builds Her Spirit

Write Isaiah 64:8 in your journal or on your bathroom mirror with a dry erase marker, and work on memorizing this verse. As you read the verse, remember that God is the Potter and you are the clay. God is willing and able to gently mold you into his likeness!

The Wise Woman Loves Her Husband

Call your mother-in-law this week just to say hello. Tell her something you appreciate about her. Let her know how much you love and value the son she raised.

The Wise Woman Loves Her Children

Enroll your children in your local library's summer reading program. Make family reading goals and read aloud every day. Also, let your children help you clean! Assign them household tasks so they can share the load. Decide what works best with your routine: small, daily chores; once a week, or a combination of the two. Give all of your children their own responsibilities. Even a child as young as three can help by sorting dirty laundry, putting away clean clothes, gathering trash from each can around the house on trash day, or helping to unload the dishwasher.

The Wise Woman Cares For Her Home

Create a snack station in your pantry and refrigerator. Designate a spot that is child-accessible and stock it with cut-up fruits, vegetables, and whatever else your children like for snacks.

"With my whole heart I seek you; let me not wander from
your commandments! I have stored up your word in my heart,
that I might not sin against you."

~ Psalm 119:10-11 (ESV)

Daily Quiet Time for Busy Mamas

By: Tara Davis

Do you struggle with prioritizing your quiet time with the Lord? With small children to care for, my time can feel especially scarce! However, my friend, you are only able to pour out to your children spiritually when you are being fed through God's Word (Psalm 119:105). If your desire is to be filled with the love of Christ, it is imperative that you spend time reading the Bible, praying, and worshiping. Your time with the Lord is important enough to make it a priority!

If you struggle in this area, here are some ideas to help:

1. **Adjust your schedule.** If quiet time isn't happening in the morning, try it at a different time of day, perhaps naptime or at night.

2. **Try an audio Bible app.** http://dailyaudiobible.com, You Version, Bible.is, or Bible Gateway are all fantastic and allow you to listen to portions of the Bible while going about your day.

3. **Baby-step your way back into the Word.** An easy-to-understand Bible version like The Message and even a good children's version like *The Jesus Storybook Bible* have both touched my heart and drawn me back into God's Word when I have felt far from the Lord.

4. **Use a good devotional as a starting point.** However, be sure to look up the Scriptures noted each day. God's Word is what feeds you (Jeremiah 15:16)!

5. **Put together quiet-time boxes for your children.** Fill these with special activities that can only come out during quiet time. Include crayons and an art notebook, puzzles, finger puppets, or play-dough.

6. **Leave your Bible open on the counter during the day.** You can read a verse or two as you have time.

7. **Pray every chance you get.** You form relationships through conversation. Start an ongoing one with the Lord today!

8. **Commit your time to the Lord.** Pray that the Holy Spirit would direct what little time you have and speak intimately to your heart (John 14:26).

9. **Involve your children.** Let your children snuggle on the couch with you as you have your time with the Lord. They will see you pursuing a relationship with Jesus, and you can share bits of what you are learning with them. Seeing real faith in action softens kids' hearts to the Lord (Deuteronomy 6:7).

Do not give up! God longs to spend time with you and will make that time count in eternal ways. Trust that, in this season, God will multiply the time you are able to give. He truly wants you to open your heart daily to Him and His message of love!

Go Deeper:

Develop a plan to encourage daily quiet time with the Lord. Implement the ideas mentioned or brainstorm others that work for you. Write your plan in your journal and pray over it, asking God to inspire you to spend time with Him.

What's Next?

It is important for your children to see you pursuing a relationship with the Lord. It is also important for them to develop a relationship with Him. Make time during the day to read and discuss God's Word with them. Buy a small journal for your children (even your little ones) in which they can write or draw about what God is speaking to their hearts.

journal

> "Yet you, Lord, are our father. We are the clay,
> you are the potter, we are all the work of your hand."
>
> ~ Isaiah 64:8

The Shaping Hands of God

By: Meagan Witt

Sweet mamas, what comes to your mind when you hear the story of the potter and the clay? This parable reminds me that God is intimately at work in every one of our lives. Throughout our lifetime, the trials, storms, and miracles are all used by God to shape and mold the deepest parts of His children's souls and minds.

This shaping process can feel overwhelming, especially when there are many areas in which we fall short or constantly think we need to overcome or improve. Sometimes, this state of our hearts can feel paralyzing, and we find ourselves feeling like a hopeless case.

If this is you, my friend, listen to the Father and allow Him to remind you of the truth from His Word. These two verses bring comfort to my soul when I feel overwhelmed by a constant need to improve:

> Come to me, all you who are weary and burdened, and I will give you rest. Take my yoke upon you and learn from me, for I am gentle and humble in heart, and you will find rest for your souls. For my yoke is easy and my burden is light."(Matthew 11:28-30)

> Ask, and it will be given to you; seek and you will find; knock and the door will be opened to you. (Matthew 7:7)

You see, friends, the Father is telling us we can come to Him and learn from Him! We can ask for more of His peace or guidance, and it will be freely given. We don't have to stress about falling short and thinking it is all up to us to improve ourselves. Doesn't that just bring joy to your heart?

As you meditate on these Scriptures, allow the overwhelming feelings of doubt, fear, and insecurity to fade away. Remember, He is the Potter, and you are the clay.

Go Deeper:

Pray and ask Jesus to continue to mold you and shape you until you look like Him.

During your time with the Lord, write down what the potter and the clay mean to you. Ask the Lord what the most important thing is for you to work on now that will help you look a little more like Him.

What's Next?

Develop a daily habit of reading Scripture. The Word of God is active and alive! Mediate on the very words of God. Allow these precious Scriptures given by the Holy Spirit and the Almighty God to encourage you as you live your life in trust. His Word will comfort you when you feel burdened.

Allow your Father to mold you as you rest in the Potter's hands, but stop trying to be perfect. *Relax* in the love of God. He is the one who brings about lasting change.

Here's an idea for your children: Give your kids some play-dough to mold and shape into whatever their hearts desire. As they are creating, use this time to read the Scriptures and talk to them about the potter and the clay.

journal

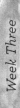

_____

_____

_____

_____

_____

_____

_____

_____

_____

_____

_____

_____

_____

_____

_____

_____

_____

_____

_____

_____

_____

_____

*"My heart is not proud, Lord, my eyes are not haughty;
I do not concern myself with great matters or things too wonderful
for me. But I have calmed and quieted myself, I am like a weaned
child with its mother; like a weaned child I am content."*

~ Psalm 131:1-2

Learning to be Still

By: Deb Weakly

Have you ever seen a nursing baby with his mother? He has moments of stillness and quiet when he rests gently in her arms, but as soon as he gets hungry, he begins to show signs of restlessness. When his mother moves to get ready to nurse, the baby starts fussing, realizing his hunger and the need for comfort.

A weaned child, on the other hand, is peaceful and content to sit on his mother's lap. Instead of crying out for the breast, he now feels satisfied to lie back, experiencing the warmth of being enveloped in mama's arms and the comfort of resting against her chest.

Dear mama, do you ever feel like a nursing baby? Does your soul feel restless and weary when you think about the uncontrollable circumstances of your life? I know mine does. Many times my heart has felt restless and discontent from the longings and unfulfilled expectations that have resided there. I found my thoughts consumed with anxiety, and my life felt out of control.

Even as I write, I sense the Holy Spirit calling me as He always does to live a surrendered life in complete humility and dependence on Christ. I feel God saying to me that I am worried about too many "many things," and I need to stop trying to control my life and my circumstances.

I am learning that only the patient love of Jesus brings true joy and peace. When I choose to give control of my life to Christ, trusting that He is good and will fulfill my longings in His way and in His timing, then I begin to see the truth: God is with me, sees me, and fulfills my heart's desires in the proper way. I see that I can't depend on people or things to make me happy. Only then can I surrender my expectations to the One who knows what's best for me and trust that He cares for me. When I count my blessings each day and see what God does give me, I find my heart happier and peaceful.

Beloved, if you find your heart in a state of restlessness and discontent, join me in asking Jesus to help us humbly turn our gaze away from ourselves and onto Him so we may feel His love and care every day. As we keep our eyes fixed on the Lord and ask Him to fill us up as only He can instead of looking to our husbands, finances, friends, or circumstances to fill our every need, we find lasting joy and the peace that surpasses understanding.

We begin to walk through each day with Jesus and waltz through each season of life with a heart of love and gratitude.

Go Deeper:

Do you have unmet expectations and desires? Release them to God and ask Him to fulfill your longings perfectly. Ask for His help to wait patiently and delight in His will. As you wait, don't miss the God-given opportunities to love others well. Seize every moment and choose to enjoy who and what He does bring.

Week Three ~ Day Three

What's Next?

Establish "check points" in your day to get into the habit of noticing the goodness of God. Involve your children and show them God is real! Upon waking and again at 9 AM, lunchtime, 3 PM, 6 PM, and bedtime, ask yourself, "Where did I see God's goodness?" Make a poster of the different times and write the little blessings in each time slot. Try this for 21 days. This one habit will change your life as you begin to feel God's presence and care in every moment of every day!

Journal

Week Three

"A new command I give you: Love one another.
As I have loved you, so you must love one another.
By this everyone will know that you are my disciples,
if you love one another."

~ John 13:34

Blessing Days

By: Krystle Porter

Want to know something that is vital for you to hear today? God loves you!

You may hear people say that in passing at church, your pastor tell the congregation, or someone say it when you are having a rough day. But *He does*! Do you need to hear that today? Is your heart heavy or burdened? His love is deep—it a jealous love—and it is a perfect love!

Listen to what this verse has to say about the way God loves you and me:

> The Lord your God is in your midst, a mighty one who will save; He will rejoice over you with gladness; he will quiet you by His love; He will exult over you with loud singing. (Zephaniah 3:17 ESV)

God has a rich, profound, joy-filled love for us. He commits each day to loving us in this way! We are so blessed! As we read in our key verse today in John 13, God wants us to extend this love to others. As mamas, He wants us to extend it to our children as well!

Love is something that needs to be intentional. It can happen naturally, but most often it is well thought out and carefully executed. I was recently talking with a sweet mom of seven about how to be a good mom, and she said, "You know what I did every day? I loved my kids. I loved them well. I spent time with them, and I told them about the Lord every opportunity I had."

To just love our children may seem very simple but it is so powerful! It is the little ways we love daily that really add up!

Go Deeper:

What are some ways that you can intentionally love your children this week? Pray and ask God to help you to be like Zephaniah in the verse above, rejoicing over your little ones, quieting their souls with your love, and exulting over them with loud singing.

What's Next?

Take a few minutes to journal. Write down a few of the ways that you have felt loved by God through the course of your life. It could be memories, experiences, or maybe promises He has kept in your heart. Write down at least five to ten!

Plan a "Blessing Day" for each of your children this summer. Choose this time to shower each individual child with your love and undivided attention. You can treat him or her, with something like a trip to get ice cream, a special movie night, or a tea-time. Show the love that you know their little soul needs. You will bless them immensely and create a lasting memory!

Put the "Blessing Days" on your calendar!

Document your time! Take a few pictures along the way, get them printed, and write a special note on the back to your child. Tell how much you enjoyed loving on that child and how special she or he is to you!

journal

_____

_____

_____

_____

_____

_____

_____

_____

_____

_____

_____

_____

_____

_____

_____

_____

_____

_____

_____

_____

_____

_____

_____

Missionaries at Home
Summer
Bingo Challenge!

By: Krystle Porter & Tara Davis

4	11	2	15
19	3	8	14
12	5	17	16
6	18	9	7
13	10	1	20

-CARD ONE-

14	10	17	6
7	4	1	13
2	18	5	19
11	20	12	8
9	3	15	16

-CARD TWO-

On Being Missionary-Minded at Home and Sharing God's Love with our Communities

We are so excited about our Help Club for Moms Summer Bingo Challenge. This time we are focused on being "Missionaries at Home!"

Oftentimes when we think of missionaries, we imagine far-off places and third world countries. However, most of us will never leave our homes and travel to these distant places. But we are still God's missionaries!

God has a mission for us, here in our own communities. We can be mission-minded at home, remembering that God has a plan for us to "go and make disciples of all nations" (Matthew 28:19a).

This summer, let's be intentional to pray for current missionaries in other countries, serve together in our own family units, and plan days and activities to shine God's love to those in our own neighborhood!

You can play this game of "Bingo" by attempting a single row, two rows or go all out for a blackout board! Be sure to share your pictures of your family completing your Bingo sheets on our Help Club for Moms Facebook page! We'd love to follow your journey and be encouraged by your faith! And remember, have FUN!

Activities are listed on the back!

~ 45 ~

Summer *Bingo* Challenge!

1. Make a missions giving box to collect spare change from your family this summer! A jar works just fine, too!

2. Write a letter of encouragement to a missionary friend!

3. Pray for God to show you where He would like your family to help in your local community (perhaps with your church or a local ministry).

4. Make a bulletin board or grab a chalkboard that you can place somewhere that gets a lot of traffic in your home. Write three ways you can pray for your local community!

5. Operation Kindness Door! Is there someone in your life that you know could use a little extra love in the season they are in? Have your kids write a few encouraging Bible verses on about 10 index cards (1 per card) and 5-10 sweet notes of encouragement on other index cards. Make sure at least one says you are praying for them! Grab some tape and tape them to their front door! What a sweet surprise to come home to!

6. Make cookies for a neighbor or two! Before you deliver them, pray for those neighbors to know the love of Jesus. Write them a short note saying you are praying for them and add a little Bible verse about God's love for them!

7. Host a movie night! Show a faith-based movie along with popcorn and other treats! Here is a short list of just a few good options: *Courageous, Soul Surfer, Luther, Fireproof, The Prayer Room...*

8. Grab some chalk! Go to a local park or even your front yard sidewalk if it's in a busy community, and write a Bible verse (John 3:16 is a great example!). Write other encouraging notes like: "God loves you!", "You are known and LOVED by God", "Believe in Jesus!". Let the kids get creative! You never know who might come across it and how God will use it for His glory!

9. Invite someone to attend church with you!

10. Make and send a care package for a missionary, someone serving in the armed forces, a homeless person, or a college student!

11. Organize a Neighborhood Help Day! Make a small flyer offering to help neighbors in need, whether it's yard work, home organization, errands, or meals. Write down your email on there as a way they can send in their requests! Spend one day this summer serving your neighbors and shining the light of Jesus!

12. Paint Rocks! Find or purchase some smooth surfaced rocks and paint them! Add Scripture verses to them or simply write "God loves you!" somewhere on the rock! Place them in your yard. Be sure to pray for your neighbor as you find a special place to put it!

13. Gather some friends and make gifts for kids in the hospital! They can be simple care packages or something crafted, and deliver them! Be sure to include a note of encouragement and share about God's love for them!

14. Help cook/serve meals at a homeless shelter!

15. Fast for one meal! Choose a people group to pray for while you fast! Keep this age-appropriate of course. Little ones will likely not understand fasting. This is meant for older children.

16. Host a small talent show and take donations! Give all donations to a local charity, homeless shelter or Christian ministry.

17. Plan an Evening of Prayer! After dinner one evening, cover the world in prayer! Put some soft worship music in the background. Have each family member put 3 things they'd like to pray for in a jar. Take turns passing the jar and praying for each and every one! Pray for different countries, people groups, government leaders. Pray for peace, for healing, for food & shelter for families, and any way that the Holy Spirit leads you! Feel free to invite others. You can even bake a special treat to enjoy once prayer time is over!

18. Choose a book to read aloud as a family over the summer about a missionary and their adventures for Christ!

19. Contact someone who is or has been a missionary and have your kids interview them to learn about their experience!

20. Memorize "The Great Commission" as a family! Matthew 28:18-20

Summer
of Joy
~ Week Four ~

Hello Dear Mamas!

I hope you are finding your summer to be refreshing and relaxing! My family and I just returned from visiting relatives out of state. We were blessed to introduce our five children to lots of family members they had never met before. My mama heart was delighted that they were surrounded by such love and acceptance. Enveloped in this type of warm homecoming, I realized the importance of nurturing extended family. Reflecting on our time together, I now desire to deepen those relationships and to keep our families connected.

Relationships matter. God's Word encourages us in 2 Corinthians 13:11, "Finally, brothers and sisters, rejoice! Strive for full restoration, encourage one another, be of one mind, live in peace."

If the Lord has planted you in a family, it is so you would not be alone. The verse above says to live at peace with each other and to strive for restoration. If you have differences with family members, pray and ask the Lord to help you forgive and make amends. I encourage you to intentionally love your immediate and extended family well. Building relationships might take effort including making phone calls, sending letters, messages, texts, pictures, or scheduling a visit. You have plenty of time to reach out and tangibly love your family well, summer isn't over yet!

With love,

Your sister Rae-Ellen Sanders and the Help Club For Moms Team

> **"***A man ought to live so that everybody knows he is a Christian...
> and most of all, his family ought to know.* **"**
> ~ D.L. Moody

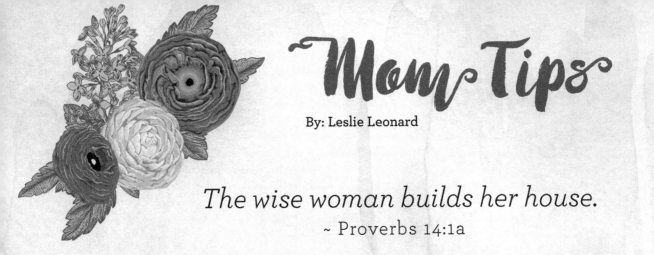

Mom Tips

By: Leslie Leonard

The wise woman builds her house.
~ Proverbs 14:1a

The Wise Woman Builds Her Spirit

Keep praise-and-worship music playing in your home this week, especially first thing in the morning. This will help set the tone for your day with your children.

The Wise Woman Loves Her Husband

Designate one night this week (and every week for the rest of the summer) to be Quiet Night. Read books, color pictures, or play a calm board game. Summer can be very busy. Slow down and spend time together as a family.

The Wise Woman Loves Her Children

Get those precious photos of your children off your phone and into albums or frames. Print some of your photos this week.

The Wise Woman Cares For Her Home

Plan your meals for the entire week by Monday morning. Make your grocery list and do all necessary shopping. List your meals here:

Monday: _____ Tuesday: _____

Wednesday: _____ Thursday: _____

Friday: _____

> "Are not two sparrows sold for a penny? Yet not one of them will fall to the ground outside your Father's care. And even the very hairs of your head are all numbered. So don't be afraid; you are worth more than many sparrows."
>
> ~ Matthew 10:29-31

God Values People

By: Jennifer Valdois

Every year, on July 4th, we Americans celebrate will celebrate our nation's Independence Day. While celebrating is fun, it is important to remember why we celebrate. Over two hundred forty years ago, Thomas Jefferson painstakingly penned the Declaration of Independence. He measured each word and weighed the consequences. Within the Declaration is one of the most well-known and timeless passages on human rights:

> We hold these truths to be self-evident, that all men are created equal, that they are endowed by their Creator with certain unalienable Rights, that among these are Life, Liberty and the pursuit of Happiness.

Every human life is valuable to God, for He created us in his image (Genesis 1:27). As we read in Matthew 10:29-31, God knows when a common sparrow falls from a tree. How much more does he care about us, His precious children? He has numbered each hair on our heads! He is an infinite God who values and instills worth into each of us; He considers us all equal.

Jesus came to proclaim good news to the poor whom He values. God sent Him "to proclaim freedom for the prisoners and recovery of sight for the blind, to set the oppressed free, to proclaim the year of the Lord's favor" (Luke 4:18). Jesus is the King of Kings, but He came to the lowly and discarded. Our God loves the poor, the refugees, the orphans, the elderly, and the oppressed women throughout our broken world.

We, too, are to respect the rights of all men by loving the "least of these" (Matthew 25:40). He tells us to feed the hungry, give drink to the thirsty, welcome the stranger, clothe the naked, care for the sick, and visit the prisoner. As God's representatives on this earth, He calls us to be his hands and feet.

This Independence Day, while you are celebrating your earthly freedoms, remember the One who made a way for you to enjoy eternal freedom and commissioned you to proclaim the Good News to the poor in this generation.

Go Deeper:

Considering we are all precious in the sight of God, how can you teach your children to share the love of Jesus with those who are hurting? Pray and ask God if there is a service project in your community where your family can serve this summer.

What's Next?

Teach your children their nation's past. Take them to the library and check out a few books about the 4th of July. I recommend *The 4th of July Story* by Alice Dalgliesh. If you are reading this in another country, find books about your national heritage! Consider inviting friends and family over for an Independence Day celebration. Plan a fun afternoon or evening. Make it a potluck!

Journal

_____
_____
_____
_____
_____
_____
_____
_____
_____
_____
_____
_____
_____
_____
_____
_____
_____
_____
_____
_____
_____
_____
_____
_____
_____
_____

"Speak and act as those who are going to be judged by the law
that gives freedom, because judgment without mercy will be shown
to anyone who has not been merciful. Mercy triumphs over judgment."
~ James 2:12-13

Unity in Christ

By: Brynne Gluch

Outrage. Disgust. Terror. Desperation for the return of Christ. These are just a few reactions I've heard, and had, in response to reports of violence in our nation, a far cry from the mercy described in the book of James.

I am a white woman and a granddaughter to two military colonels. To say my family has a sincere regard toward those who serve our country in uniform would be an understatement. I am also an adoptive mother of an African-American son. I will admit that fear floods my heart when I see on the news that our culture seems to be drawing a line in the sand and picking sides that leave no option for a blended-race family.

At first, I didn't know how to respond to the many tragedies that have occurred as a result of racial tension. My limited perspective as the mother of an infant black son carries a sense of embarrassment because I know this is not a new issue for many other women.

But I am his mom, and with God's grace, I have to face my own blind spots.

"Be completely humble and gentle; be patient, bearing with one another in love. Make every effort to keep the unity of the Spirit through the bond of peace" (Ephesians 4:2-3).

At church a few Sundays ago, something clicked in my heart. The pastor asked us to turn to our neighbor and pray for our nation. I joined hands with the woman next to me and began to pray. She started praying for her son whom she mentioned serves as a police officer. The fear she was feeling for his life was apparent in her voice and tone. I took a deep breath and began to pray for my son and the fear I feel for him growing up in a white family that has never experienced racial prejudice or oppression. This woman and I looked up at each other, and there was this realization that we're both just scared moms, but that we're on the same team. We squeezed hands and sat back in our seats.

"Come to me, all who are weary and heavy-laden, and...you will find rest for your souls...for my burden is light" (Matthew 11:28-30 NASB).

Fear can be an effective tactic of the enemy if we allow it to be. If we stay afraid, we remain divided. So, the enemy is on a mission to keep us scared. Our natural reaction to feeling threatened is called "fight or flight" by which we either pursue our justice in anger, or hide and isolate ourselves (Been there!). But God's ways are higher than our ways, and there is so much freedom in choosing forgiveness, peace, and mercy, just as Christ did while being crucified.

"Bear one another's burdens, and thereby fulfill the law of Christ" (Galatians 6:2 NASB).

The paradoxical nature of Scripture leaves no room for rigid legalism. God is not asking us to sit on our hands. On the contrary, He calls us to do something! The apostle Paul reminds us that we are no longer circumcised and uncircumcised, but that we can experience radical unity because Jesus died for us. Peace requires us to surrender our right to be justified and own what we can in repentance.

"Great faith doesn't come out of great effort, but out of great surrender. Faith doesn't deny a problem's existence. It denies it a place of influence." – Pastor Bill Johnson

Go Deeper:

There's good news: the Father of all nations is just a prayer away. In a posture of humility, ask the Lord to search your heart for misunderstanding or unforgiveness. Hurt people respond by hurting other people, so it is imperative that we tend to the garden of our hearts. The Holy Spirit will help us understand and heal. If the news is causing you to fear or stir up an offense, turn it off and ask God to share with you His hope-filling news!

What's Next?

Seek to understand. Love and listen to someone different. We all have a unique story. We must not assume we know where other people are coming from when they speak up about hard issues. Sisters, let's not let fear keep us silent. Let's be brave. **Let's ask more questions and offer fewer opinions.** Let's be known for our love and amazing testimonies of reconciliation.

journal

"Teach us to number our days,
that we may gain a heart of wisdom."
~ Psalm 90:12

Check Yourself Before You Wreck Yourself

By: Deb Weakly

For the past year, I have had a little handwritten sign inside my teacup cabinet that reads, "What would I do if I only had one year to live?" I like to keep this thought in front of me each day as I grab my china teacup for my morning time with God, and then get ready for my day.

When I see this little sign, I ask myself some questions: How would I live my life *today* if I only had one year to live? Who or what would be most important to me? Would I choose to overlook offenses or give grace? Would I choose to love well?

I think about these questions a lot. To be honest, I can frequently wake up with negative thoughts about someone or something and it can steal my joy for the day right off the bat. Pondering these questions helps me to "check myself before I wreck myself," and helps me get my day off to a more positive start.

Instead of dwelling on negative thoughts and becoming grouchy, anxious, or needy, I pray and practice 2 Corinthians 10:5b by "...taking every thought captive to the obedience of Christ." I give that negative, toxic thought to Jesus and ask Him to help me think a true thought about the person or situation. This one habit has helped me to catch myself before those thoughts run their course for the day and affect my relationships with others. I can ask Jesus to help me to choose to live and love in the power of the Holy Spirit. This one little habit has increased my joy tremendously.

I don't always do this perfectly, but I do keep trying. I figure if I can check myself 300 days out of the 365 each year, then I am doing a whole lot better than if I didn't try to change my thoughts at all. I love how Dory the Fish says: "Just keep swimming. Just keep swimming." I keep trying to do better each day, and not give up even if I don't always do it perfectly.

Another joy-increasing habit I have been doing for years is praying Psalm 90:12, asking Jesus to teach me to number my days so I can go about my day in His wisdom. When we live each day as if our days are numbered, we live with purpose and joy.

Sister, our lives are so short, and the Lord wants us to live them to the fullest with His Spirit leading the way. So how about you? Would you like to live each day with more joy? Try checking yourself first thing in the morning and also asking Jesus to teach you to number your days. These little habits can help you to savor your days and live each day as if you only had a short time on this earth.

Go Deeper:

Pray and ask Jesus if there are any toxic thoughts going through your mind. If He brings something to mind, write it down. Then ask Him for a true thought about your situation and write that one down. It could be a Scripture or a simple prayer such as "Jesus, please protect me and my family." Or, if you're struggling in the area of finances, you could say, "Thank you, Jesus, that my God will meet all *my* needs according to the riches of his glory in Christ Jesus" (Philippians 4:19).

What's Next?

Count your days! I once heard of a man who wanted to appreciate his life and decided to number his days. He counted up how many Sundays he had left if he lived to be 85 years old, and bought that number of marbles and put them in a jar. Each Sunday, he took out a marble to remind him that he had just lived one week of his life. He spoke at our church about how this habit changed him and helped him to appreciate his life more. I think it would affect our lives too!

Journal

"Keep on loving one another as brothers and sisters.
Do not forget to show hospitality to strangers, for by so doing
some people have shown hospitality to angels without knowing it."

~ Hebrews 13:1-2

The Art of Christian Hospitality

By: Mari Jo Mast

"The heart of hospitality is about creating space for someone to feel seen and heard and loved. It's about declaring your table a safe zone, a place of warmth and nourishment." – Shauna Nicquest

I admit, I often cringe and feel intimidated when I hear the word "hospitality." God challenges me in this area continually! I have a lot of flesh to conquer and misconceptions to let go of in the area of hospitality. I also realize I have missed out on a lot of blessings because I focus on my own silly ideals. Perfectionism can be my downfall. Do you struggle too?

This has made me wonder: what does hospitality truly mean?

I remember my parents talking fondly of my dad's parents. Since they were missionaries and pastors to a small Mennonite church, guests and friends would arrive unannounced to visit their home any time of day. Sometimes complete strangers, friends of friends, were traveling out of state and needed a place to stay for the night. No matter who they were, my grandparents were always ready and would graciously invite them inside and provide them with a snack or home-cooked meal, no matter how inconvenient it was for them. Often, they would offer a clean room and warm bed with an invitation to stay the night. Turning anyone away was simply out of the question. Oh, to live like this!

I also have a sweet friend who loves hospitality. She makes authentic and simple servanthood look easy; I tell her it is a gift. Her home, though very beautiful, never takes the spotlight. Guests feel appreciated when they enter, and the food she creates, though simple, is nourishing and plenteous. I believe she prays over it, and I have secretly wondered how it seems to multiply! The fellowship and prayer we have in her home always bring an atmosphere of love and peace. Those who eat at her table come away knowing it was a holy experience, having tangibly felt the presence of God.

Leaving her home inspires me. I want my serving to be a form of worship around the table like hers, where guests create heart-to-heart connection and unforgettable, fond memories. Both examples humble me. Both are a picture of true hospitality.

Years ago, hospitality was a normal and regular part of life, but let's be honest; slowly and surely, times have changed. It's common now to refer guests and friends alike to a hotel or restaurant nearby instead of welcoming them into our homes when we are unprepared, but I think we are missing out on a blessing when we neglect opportunities for hospitality.

Hebrews 13:2 (BBE) has something interesting to say about allowing our homes to be accessible to anyone at any time: "Take care to keep open house: Because in this way some have had angels as guests, without being conscious about it." Hospitality must be important to God for the Bible to say that. It sounds like it should be a normal part of our lives. I'm asking God to change my heart and my desires.

Week Four ~ Day Four

So, instead of cringing and being intimidated, I'm trying to choose humility. It's a breath of fresh air when I see things are not perfect (dirty dishes in the sink, mounds of laundry, little handprints on the windows) when I enter a home. Maybe allowing others to see my mess gives them the freedom to do the same. And if my home doesn't resemble "House Beautiful," it doesn't matter. It's not about my house anyway! Will you join me?

Below are simple guidelines on what hospitality should and should not be about. This helps shed light on some lies you and I may personally believe that keep us from serving and opening up our home. Maybe they can help us focus on what is truly important!

What Hospitality Should Not be About:

- **Your house:** It should never be the focus, only the space where love and sweet fellowship happen.
- **Performance:** Don't go out of your way to do things or make foods you normally wouldn't! Be yourself! If you don't do it with your kids, don't do it with guests.
- **Perfection:** If the house is a little messy, don't stress. If the burgers are overcooked, it's totally okay!
- **A time to impress:** Don't let your food or decorating distract you from serving, listening, and loving. Don't try to impress your guests; let your focus be on them, not you.

What Hospitality Is About:

- **Simplicity:** Hosting is about the experience, not the appearance. Make a simple meal that lets you fully enjoy your guests. You can use your regular dishes or fancy china, whatever you feel is suitable for the occasion. Sometimes it's alright to ask guests to bring a dish!
- **Authenticity:** Again, be yourself. This liberates others to be themselves, too! Don't hide anything, and remove all masks.
- **Relationship and godly love:** Ask for God's heart to truly be able to love and relate to your guests. 1 Corinthians 13 is a fantastic guide to hospitality. Read it before your guests arrive.
- **Celebration:** Thank God for divine appointments with your friends and guests. Embrace it when it happens. Food, of course, is always included when we celebrate! Ask God what meal you should make, keeping nutrition and nourishment in mind.
- **Prepare your kids:** Let them know what will take place ahead of time. Hosting can be difficult with children, but if your children have an idea of what you expect, it will be easier for everyone. Remember to include them in your conversation!
- **Prayer:** Nothing binds relationships together like prayer. Remember this and bless your guests before they leave.

Go Deeper:

The atmosphere of your home cannot be imitated. Make it a place where friends and guests feel welcome and appreciated for who they are. Let it be a natural place, where relaxed friendships and pleasant conversations can happen. Let's open our minds and hearts to be the change our culture needs! Let's facilitate a place of authenticity and love in our homes, ministering to tired souls in need of refreshment.

What's Next?

1. Pray about who you could invite into your home within the next few weeks.
2. Prepare your heart to open your home to any strangers.
3. Send out an invitation!
4. Purpose in your heart to keep everything simple. Be authentic and celebrate your time together when your guests arrive.
5. Remember to allow your kids to be a part of the fun!

Journal

_____
_____
_____
_____
_____
_____
_____
_____
_____
_____
_____
_____
_____
_____
_____
_____
_____
_____
_____
_____
_____
_____
_____
_____
_____
_____
_____
_____

Week Four

Food for the Soul

This Summer Berry Tart is SIMPLE and a SHOWSTOPPER at the same time! Perfect for the Fourth of July, a family reunion or a barbecue in the backyard. Not only is it colorful and impressive to look at, but it is also seriously easy to make. The only thing that takes an effort in this recipe is the tart shell and even that is stress-free. The filling is no-bake so it is not time-consuming.

I love custard, don't get me wrong, but this recipe calls for a faux custard (no boiling and cooling) by using Mascarpone Cheese found in the special cheese section in most grocery stores. It is a delicate type of cream cheese and highly recommended to get this unique flavor. By whipping cream until peaks form, you still get the same creamy goodness typical in traditional custards. When added to the cheese and other ingredients, it becomes a delightful substitution. Flavor the cream by adding zest from either a lemon or an orange—it really enhances the flavor! This recipe is customizable; you choose what zest to add and what jam to use as a glaze. The inner artist in you shines when you get to design the berries on top.

SUMMER BERRY TART By: Rae-Ellen Sanders

Ingredients for Topping:

Fresh berries: blackberries, blueberries, raspberries, strawberries—washed, dried, hulled, and sliced

½ cup jam of choice: apricot, strawberry, orange marmalade

2 Tbsp. water

Crust:

2 cups flour of choice: white, almond, whole grain

½ cup Confectioner's sugar

1 tsp. salt

1 tsp. vanilla extract

8 Tbsp. butter cut into pieces

Directions:

1. Whisk together the flour and salt, set aside.

2. With an electric mixer, cream the butter, sugar and vanilla extract.

3. Blend together on low speed. Add up to 2 tablespoons of water if too dry.

4. Shape into a ball, wrap with plastic wrap and refrigerate (the longer the better).

5. Meanwhile, cut a large enough circle of Parchment paper and insert in your tart pan—you will want to do this step for easy removal. Spray the sides with cooking spray and when your oven is preheated to 350 degrees, roll out and press dough into the bottom and up the sides of a tart pan.

6. Using a fork, prick the bottom in several areas to prevent bubbles, and bake for 10-15 minutes till slightly brown. That wasn't so hard, right? Whip up your faux custard while you let your crust cool.

Food for the Soul

Faux Custard:

8 ounces of Mascarpone Cheese

2 cups heavy whipping cream

1 tsp. vanilla extract

¼ cup Confectioner's sugar

1-2 tsp. grated zest (lemon, orange)

Directions:

1. Mix Mascarpone Cheese (it is already soft in the container—so do not microwave or heat) with sugar, the zest and vanilla extract. Set aside.

2. Whip the cream with a blender until peaks form.

3. Gently fold in together and spread inside the crust.

4. Now you are ready to decorate with berries in whatever pattern you like. You can't mess this part up—it looks divine no matter how you layer the fruit.

5. The last step is to make a glaze by heating your jam with 2 tablespoons of water in the microwave or stove-top until syrupy.

6. Allow the jam to cool and then brush over fruit.

7. Refrigerate until ready to serve. Make sure to take pictures before indulging in your creamy and surprisingly sweet perfection!

Summer of Joy

~ Week Five ~

Dear Mama,

Your children are growing up so quickly—enjoy every minute you have with them. Though you may not hear it from important people in our culture today, what you are doing is the MOST important job in the world! Your endless serving of your family is an ETERNAL investment only a heavenly God can fully notice and reward. You are filling and storing up treasures in HEAVEN as you selflessly love and give.

The older I get, the more I realize "motherhood" is a precious gift from The Lord, a beautiful treasure with an eternal reward from His gracious hand. We are wise to be thankful for this opportunity as mothers! Let's purpose in our hearts to embrace everything it has to offer. As we give it our best shot, we can trust God to bring forth beautiful, lasting fruit from our intentional labor.

With love,

Mari Jo Mast and the Help Club for Moms Team

> *If you are wise and understand God's ways,*
> *prove it by living an honorable life, doing good works*
> *with the humility that comes from wisdom.*
> *~ James 3:13 (NLT)*

Mom Tips

By: Leslie Leonard

The wise woman builds her house.
~ Proverbs 14:1a

The Wise Woman Builds Her Spirit

Pray 1 Corinthians 13:4-5, 7-8 each day this week. Ask God to help you love well. If you are having trouble having a regular quiet time with God, pray and ask God to help you. Use the weekly plan sheet at end of this book and write in your week's schedule and times for your Bible study each day. Start with short, 15-minute quiet times. Ask God to help you to stay focused this week, and make time with God a priority.

The Wise Woman Loves Her Husband

Plan a date night with your husband this week. If your budget allows a babysitter and a night out, take advantage of the time alone together. If not, plan a special evening at home, after the children are tucked in for the night. Play a board game, watch a favorite movie, or try your hand at a Pinterest DIY project together.

The Wise Woman Loves Her Children

Read the Bible with your children this week. Set aside one or two afternoons to read aloud from the Word. Let your children color pictures while you read. This simple activity will help them fidget less while they are listening.

The Wise Woman Cares For Her Home:

Visit your local farmers market. This is a great way to save money on your grocery budget, try new foods, and support your local businesses. My family often plans a day around it, and my children enjoy looking at crafts and tasting samples.

> "The tongue can bring death or life;
> those who love to talk will reap the consequences."
>
> ~ Proverbs 18:2 (NLT)

The Power of the Tongue

By: Kara Schrock

One particularly stressful day, I firmly plopped my little guy down on the bathroom counter, looked into his eyes, and said, "Why do you have to be such a bad boy?"

I had no idea of the power of my words. As I lay on my bed that night, I talked to God:

Father, show me what it means to bless, and teach me how to speak life into my babies' hearts.

What words have been spoken over me by others that I have received deep into my heart? Father, please show me your truth instead so I can replace these curses with the truth of your Word. Heal my heart so I can live well.

Depression hounded my family lineage for as long as I can remember. As a little girl, I knelt next to my bed, praying, begging God for healing and answers to our family curse. Years later, God answered me on that stressful day.

The answer came in the wilted face of my 3-year-old son as God whispered deeply into my heart, "Kara, the root of depression stems from verbal abuse. It traps both the one speaking and the one listening."

My world stood still in the darkness that night as I inclined my heart to understand what God had spoken to me. For days, my heart repented. I grieved and mourned the damaging words I had spoken throughout the years. I searched Scripture to see if this was true, if I really was causing damage with my words, and here is what I found:

Fathers, do not exasperate your children; instead, bring them up in the training and instruction of the Lord. (Ephesians 6:4)

Out of the same mouth come praise and cursing. My brothers and sisters, this should not be. (James 3:10)

Dear mama, I'm writing you today to refresh your weary soul! I'm here to tell you what I wish someone would have shared with me years ago: there is a better way! Words shape and form your child's identity. When you bless your child with words of love and encouragement, it will empower her or him to become what you speak!

Love needs no defense, not even words of defense. Be patient and kind; your child does not have power over evil, but you do! Show your child the way! Look beyond the behavior and see the pain of the child. Many people react because of hurt in their hearts. For example, if children feel left out, they may respond by destroying the tower they could not help build. Ask the Holy Spirit to show you what caused the behavior in the first place. Actions begin to change when children's hearts feel ministered to and when the truth is spoken.

Go Deeper:

Rescue your children from themselves. Children are like adults in that, after we've had a bad day, isolation— like timeout for a child—may not help us feel better. What helps us moms rather than condemnation is for our husbands to hold us for a while or take us out for a treat. Apply this principle to your children. Sit down, open your arms toward them, and hold them close. Sometimes this may be enough, but other times you may want to add a change of scenery and go for a milkshake date. Reassure them of your love! Mom, let me tell you, this works!

What's Next?

Father God wants to speak even more to you today, so take a few minutes, step into His presence, and let Him hold you. He knows your innermost pain and struggles. Let Him speak peace over your storms. He will tell you exactly what your babies need, but let Him fill your cup first. You get to choose life today. You get to love and be loved by the most forgiving and unconditional love a mom could ever know, the love of your Heavenly Father and your dear babies! Don't push away the moment; embrace it.

Scripture References:

- Deuteronomy 30:19   • Matthew 12:37   • 1 Peter 3:9   • Proverbs 11:25

Journal

> "...the God who gives life to the dead and speaks of things that don't yet exist as if they are real."
>
> ~ Romans 4:17b (ERV)

Expect Great Things

By: Deb Weakly

A while back, a friend of mine encouraged me to do the "Love your Spouse Challenge" on Facebook. I was surprised at how much I enjoyed it—even more than I thought I would! While sharing my posts, I wrote all the things I loved about my husband at each stage of our relationship. Pondering how we met and all of the fun we've had together over the past 28 years made me smile at my husband a little more, and my heart felt happier than usual thinking about our great life together! I think that's the key to being happy; we remember the good, and we expect the good, especially from God!

When we expect great things from God and other people, we often get what we're looking for: great things! But if we allow ourselves to stay in a place of doubt and look for all of the things that are wrong in our relationships with God and the people in our lives, we will stay in that place of unbelief and experience the fruit of a faithless life. This type of life does not please God, and this lack of trust and faith affects our relationship with Him and others.

Even when we don't feel God helping us or changing a situation, rest assured, He hears every prayer and will answer in the perfect time that He himself knows to be best. Our faith is very precious to God, and He wants us to show faith constantly while we are praying and waiting on His wisdom, answers, and help.

I remember when my daughter, Christie, was younger and incredibly strong-willed! It seemed as if she was constantly in trouble, and my heart prayed and cried out to God day and night for help and wisdom! During this time, my husband was reading *The Sacred Romance* by John Eldridge. Through this book, he became aware of the power of focusing on the good in people and seeing them as who they could become, not as who they presently are. We both agreed to apply this principle of speaking of things that don't yet exist as if they are real (Romans 4:17 ERV), to our daughter. I believe this one habit changed our relationships with our daughter and set the stage for the beautiful, close relationship we all enjoy as a family now. Speaking life is powerful!

Our words have power, and they show our faith or lack of faith in God and the members of our family and friends. Was my daughter perfect all the time, or did God answer my prayers by giving us only easy days from then on? Certainly not! But we began to treat Christie like she was the sweet, godly, purpose-driven person she could become. We spoke words of faith, not because of anything Christie would do or accomplish or whether she would obey. We based our words on the belief that God and His faithfulness and power could help make her into the Christ-follower and amazing woman she is today.

That's the key: speak words of faith and life to the people and situations in your lives as if the outcome depends on God, His power, and the promises in Scripture. Base your words of faith on God answering your prayers, no matter how long it takes. I'm not saying you should live in denial or be blind to your child's sin or the problems in your life, but I am saying you should "call into being" the possibilities in your child's life or your situation.

Go Deeper:

Pray and ask God to give you a list of encouraging words you can speak over your husband and children. Write them in your journal and use them for the "What's Next" exercise below.

What's Next?

Do you have a difficult spouse or child? How about, instead of complaining about him to God or your friends, praying for him! Then believe God is answering your prayers and act as if He is answering right now! Catch your difficult child being good as much as possible! Praise your husband and tell him how much you love and appreciate him. Live your life as if God is making the changes and answering your prayers. Call the greatness into being with your words.

Does this require humility? You bet! Your husband may not be encouraging, or your teen may be rude. Even so, be kind and trust God. Remember, you are not placing your trust in people and their behavior; you are placing your trust and hope in the living God, the One who made the heavens and the earth and is faithful to answer!

Journal

_____

_____

_____

_____

_____

_____

_____

_____

_____

_____

_____

_____

_____

_____

_____

"The Spirit of God has made me,
and the breath of the Almighty gives me life."
~ Job 33:4

Just Breathe

By: Leslie Leonard

Recently, I traveled on an airplane with my two daughters. The gate agent called our zone, and we boarded the plane. We found our row of seats, settled in for our flight, and put headphones on as the plane took off. It was the beginning of a very routine day of air travel, mundane even. But what happened next was anything but mundane.

I had a severe asthma attack on the plane. I could not breathe. As I gasped for breath, desperately looking for my rescue inhaler, I knew I was slowly losing control. Two things made this situation seem hopeless: my rescue inhaler was on the bathroom countertop at my home, and everyone around me was whispering about me. At least my girls were blissfully unaware, watching *Zootopia* on their iPads while I was convinced I was going to die on that airplane. I thought to myself: *Is this it Jesus? Is this where it all ends? On an airplane surrounded by strangers?*

After 10 minutes (it felt like a lifetime), I finally got my breathing under control. Tears streamed down my face, and I hoped people were no longer staring at me. I sat in my seat and prayed to God, thanking Him for helping me in my time of need.

Dear sisters, I learned a powerful lesson on that airplane; no matter what I think, I am never in control. I often believe the hype the media sells us: that I am in complete control of my life and destiny. This is a bold-faced lie from Satan himself. God is always in control. Matthew 8:23-27 reminds us of God's sovereignty and His ability to maintain control. The disciples allowed fear to rule instead of faith. I urge you to walk in faith with God and allow Him to actively have control in your life.

I don't know what you are currently facing right now. Maybe you are dealing with a particularly difficult child, a scary medical diagnosis, or your husband turning away from you emotionally or physically. It is my hope to encourage you today that, even if your life feels completely out of control, God sees you for who you are and loves you. He is in complete control of your life.

No matter what you face in your life, you can take comfort in the fact that God is in control.

For further study, read the following verses:

- Deuteronomy 10:14
- Job 42:2
- Psalm 103:19
- Isaiah 45:6-7
- Zephaniah 3:17
- Revelation 21:6

Go Deeper:

What area of your life do you tend to control or micromanage? How does it make you feel and the people in your life feel? I challenge you to let go of control for one week in an area you identified. Give it over to God and fully trust in Him to fulfill/meet your expectations. Journal and pray every day to help ease your anxiety and emotions.

Week Five

What's Next?

Let's make a choice together. Let's choose God first, sisters. Together, we can make a deliberate choice to recognize the sovereignty of God in our homes, marriages, and lives.

I would love to hear about the miracles that happen in your life when you choose to put God first. I hope you share on the website or on our Facebook page.

Journal

_____

_____

_____

_____

_____

_____

_____

_____

_____

_____

_____

_____

_____

_____

_____

_____

_____

_____

_____

_____

_____

Week Five

"My grace is always more than enough for you,
and my power finds its full expression through your weakness."

~ 2 Corinthians 12:9 (TPT)

Overcoming Mommy Guilt

By: Brynne Gluch

We live in the digital age of information overload, which has brought with it a sweeping epidemic of overwhelmed millennial mamas—myself included. It's nothing new that when a woman gets pregnant, she receives a lot of advice. This truth has been magnified for the first generation of mothers to be connected by the internet. A whole world of "commenters" can now chime in on the often already opposing opinions of parents and peers on the virtues of motherhood. It's scary as a first-time mom to think that motherhood is such a moving target; how will we ever know if we're doing it right?

So we try and do it all. Sayings like, "This mama runs on coffee and wine," or "Don't talk to me, I'm potty training," are memes commonly found on social media and graphic T's sold at Target or Etsy. While these shirts are hilarious (and I want one), I believe they expose a broader issue: we as mothers need support more than instruction, and an injection of grace.

As strong women determined to do what it takes to be the best moms for our kids, it's easy to fall into the trap of perfectionism. We burn the candle at both ends trying to do it all, losing our individualized identity and sleep, and inevitably we burn out. So, what's the answer?

Jesus. The answer is always Jesus.

The good news of the Gospel is that it offers the grace injection we need to relieve the pressure to perform as mothers. Our key verse today shows that Jesus takes it one step further, saying that we need to embrace our weaknesses. What a perspective shift!

I want to share with you how that truth moved from my head to my heart. After 18 months of spending every waking moment trying to preserve my firstborn daughter from any form of toxin, non-organic food, interrupted sleep, or emotional discomfort, a horrible thing happened: she burned her hand on our fireplace cover. I was a mess, and I couldn't forgive myself for not running fast enough to grab her before she severely burned her hands. How could I let this happen? As her mother, I was supposed to meet her every need and protect her from any harm.

God spoke to my heart through 1 John 3:20, "If our hearts condemn us, we know that God is greater than our hearts, and he knows everything." He was not condemning my error. He also reminded me that, during premarital counseling, I had learned that my husband and I were not created to meet each other's every need, because some needs would only be able to be met by God. Likewise, I realized that I was not created to meet all of my child's needs, but that there needed to be room for her to need Jesus.

I pulled my sweet bandaged baby close and whispered to her, "Mama loves you, but she will make mistakes and let you down, and as much as she will try not to, but God is always here for you, and

He will never let you down." She couldn't understand me, but speaking that over her lifted the heavy weight of perfectionism off my shoulders. God showed me that my shortcomings were an opportunity for me to model dependency on Christ, not a cause for self-condemnation.

We aren't meant to be perfect for our kids, but rather to point them toward a perfect God who is willing and able to give them all the desires of their heart.

Our relationship with Jesus gives us the power to say NO to shame, and YES to the abundant life He promised in the book of John 10:10b, "I have come that they may have life, and have it to the full."

I pray this helps you feel empowered to fully live.

Go Deeper:

Did this devotional resonate with your heart? How? What do you feel the Holy Spirit speaking to you in response to what you just read?

What's Next?

Look at your calendar, and prioritize some time alone. As busy moms, it won't happen if we don't plan it ahead of time!

This may expose some mommy-guilt, but press on—you cannot overcome shame without grace, and the giver of grace is Jesus himself. I pray that as you steal away for some time with Him, that you will be filled with the fullness of his UNCONDITIONAL love for you.

journal

Start a *Breakfast Basket* Routine!

By: Tara Davis

"Love the Lord your God with all your heart and with all your soul and with all your strength. These commandments that I give you today are to be on your hearts. Impress them on your children. Talk about them when you sit at home and when you walk along the road, when you lie down and when you get up." – Deuteronomy 6:4-7

Do you struggle to find time to intentionally share Jesus with your kids? Let me tell you a little secret about what works in our house: Food. My kids are a captive audience any time they are eating! During mealtime they happily soak up the Bible, kids devotions, and hymn stories. They will readily recite Bible passages, sing praises to Jesus, think of things they are thankful for, pray fervently, and listen to stories about great Christian men and women.

I keep a basket of books by our table so I have everything I need at my fingertips (we call it our morning time basket, but choose a meal that works for you if mornings are too busy). This is an easy habit, and I can tell it's making an impact on their little hearts and lives. Maybe this is a fun habit for you to try this summer!

Some of our favorite morning time books are listed here. Your local library or thriftbooks.com are great resources for cheap or free books!

- *The Jesus Storybook Bible* – Sally Lloyd Jones
- *Answers In Genesis Answer Books for Kids* set – Ken Ham
- *Leading Little Ones to God* – Marian Schoolland
- *My Big Book of Five Minute Devotions* – Pamela Kennedy
- *The Action Bible* – Doug Mauss
- *Hero Tales* – Dave Jackson
- *The Child's Story Bible* – Catherine Vos
- *Dusty's Beary Tales* – Ruthann Winans
- *Hymns For a Kid's Heart* – Joni Eareckson Tada
- *Kingdom Tales* – David and Karen Mains
- *Case For Faith For Kids* – Lee Strobel
- *Little People Set* – Kenneth Taylor

Summer of Joy

~ Week Six ~

Dear Sweet Mama,

As I sit and reflect on when I was overdue with my baby boy, I remember what a tough season that was. My mom was in town awaiting her grandson's arrival, and he just wouldn't come! I was anxious and unsettled.

However, it is in those times that we need to quiet our hearts especially before the Lord. Lately, He has been speaking to me, reminding me to release my worries and concerns to Him unceasingly. Seasons of waiting are hard, and I often find myself questioning what the Lord is trying to teach me during those times.

Can't we all agree that waiting is difficult? It is not fun and often doesn't seem to make sense. An encouraging verse I like to keep close to my heart amid the waiting is Lamentations 3:25 (ESV): "The LORD is good to those who wait for him, to the soul who seeks him."

The Lord wants us to wait. We grow when we wait, and most importantly, we lean on Him and rely on His strength when we wait. Ultimately, He wants our souls to seek Him.

Are you waiting for something this summer? Do you desire comfort or relief from an issue or weakness in your life? Dear mama, I would love to challenge you today to go to the foot of the Cross. You will find strength for your soul there and a respite from your weariness and impatience.

Trust me in that I know how you are feeling, and we will get through this season together.

God bless you and your family!

With love,

Rachel Jones and the Help Club For Moms Team

> *What God does in us while we wait is as important as what it is we are waiting for.*
> ~ John Ortberg

Mom Tips

By: Leslie Leonard

The wise woman builds her house.
~ Proverbs 14:1a

The Wise Woman Builds Her Spirit

Journal the following questions this week: What are my strengths? What are my values? What is my proudest accomplishment?

The Wise Woman Loves Her Husband

Call or text your husband at work this week. Let him know he was on your mind and that you love him. Simply take a moment out of your day to encourage your husband, asking nothing in return. You and he will feel blessed! Also, try to get out of the habit of criticizing your husband. Take a day this week and go the entire day without criticizing his actions. This simple change in thought will bless both of you and strengthen your marital bond.

The Wise Woman Loves Her Children

When disciplining your kids this week, try to use words of affirmation. Instead of saying, "Stop whining right now," say, "You look upset. Do you need a hug?" Also, when saying "Yes" or "No" this week, make it a point to let the decision stand. Do not go back on your word. Let your yes mean yes, and your no mean no.

The Wise Woman Cares For Her Home

Straighten up and clean out your linen closet. Donate or throw away any towels and sheets you no longer use. Consider downsizing the amount of linens you keep on hand.

"...But my righteous one will live by faith.
And I take no pleasure in the one who shrinks back."

~ Hebrews 10:38

Stop Scrolling and Start Believing

By: Deb Weakly

Do you ever feel bombarded by images of a perfect marriage? Simply scrolling down our social media feed on any given day can cause us to feel envious of posts shared showing perfect husbands and happy wives. These pictures can cause us to compare our husband or our family to our social media friends, and we may even find ourselves thinking, "Her husband bought her flowers for no reason. Why doesn't my husband do that for me?" or "They really look like a happy family. I wish my family was happier."

This comparison trap happened to me several years ago, and I am happy to say that I chose to unfollow some of my "friends" on social media because I grew weary of their "perfect" lives with their "perfect" families. I needed to guard my heart against unrealistic expectations for my life and my family. I am thankful to God for showing me a powerful truth: When we bite the apple of comparison, we dangerously begin to expect our husband or kids to perform or love us in certain ways, and that is downright unfair to them. Sister, let's be honest for a moment. Most of us have certain expectations for our lives, but if these dreams and desires don't line up with what God wants for our family, we are selling ourselves short of God's best, and we will be sorely disappointed.

I knew I needed to stop complaining, so I began praying more fervently for my husband, and tried to stop focusing on things I wished he would change, and started looking for the good things he was doing instead. I began listening to him more and telling him how proud I was of him for something he was doing well. This really, really encouraged Randy and he even shared how much it meant to him that I was simply listening to him, instead of criticizing him for being grouchy. During this season, I learned there is power in the thoughts we think and the words we say about our husband and kids.

I once heard a story of a woman who made a tape recording of the positive things she loved about her husband and her marriage, and played them each morning while getting ready. Her husband was also getting ready at the same time and heard these positive things said about him and their marriage. I am sure that he must have felt cynical at first and doubted whether she meant the words that she spoke. Over time, though, their marriage got better and began to heal. Yes! Our words have power!

Today's Scripture speaks powerfully of God's desire for His children to live by faith. Do you ever think about what it means to *live* by faith? Living by faith means daily laying down our expectations for our lives and choosing to trust God and keep going, even when life gets hard. We show our faith by the thoughts we think, the words we say, and by placing our hope and trust in God. We live by faith in our marriage when we thank God for the things that are going *right*, instead of grumbling about our hurts and disappointments. I challenge you to focus where you want to go in your marriage, and not where you don't want to go. Look for the good, my friend, and you will begin to find it, and your joy will increase.

Week Six ~ Day One

Week Six

Go Deeper:

Take a moment right now and ask the Holy Spirit if you are comparing your husband or children to anyone else. If the answer is "Yes," then hold old your hands and visualize yourself giving those thoughts to Jesus. Ask Him to help your relationships with your husband and kids to improve.

What's Next?

Proverbs 18:21a says, "The tongue has the power of life and death..." Your words have power and you should use them for good!

Download a voice recording app on your phone and say out loud ten things you love about your husband. You can even say, "Thank you God that my husband is _____." That way, it's a prayer of thanksgiving to the Lord about your husband. Listen to that recording over and over as you get ready in the morning. Watch this one habit change the way you feel about your man!

Journal

_____

_____

_____

_____

_____

_____

_____

_____

_____

_____

_____

_____

_____

_____

_____

_____

_____

_____

_____

_____

"Let your eyes look directly forward,
and your gaze be straight before you.
Ponder the path of your feet;
then all your ways will be sure.
Do not swerve to the right or to the left;
turn your foot away from evil."

~ Proverbs 4:25-27 (ESV)

Walking the Path God has for You

By: Carmen Brown

All my life I have looked to others for validation, wondering if I am doing things right and if I measure up as a mom. The Lord has been teaching me over the past few years, though, that I need to look to Him and listen for His still, small voice to guide me into what is right for my family and me. I have found that comparison kills my ability to be the best God wants me to be. When I constantly turn to the right or the left, comparing myself to others, I can't see what God has for me.

"And your ears shall hear a word behind you saying, 'this is the way, walk in it,' when you turn to the right or when you turn to the left" (Isaiah 30:21). This verse talks about walking a path. Sometimes we come to a fork in the road, and we don't know which way to turn. But we can trust His voice, His Word, to guide us. We are never to swerve to the right or the left, which, according to the verse above, can turn our feet toward evil. We are never to lose sight of this path by allowing distractions to get in the way of seeing it clearly.

If you imagine a car swerving, you can imagine someone out of control and going too fast. This is how we feel when obstacles and scary times come our way, but the Lord will guide us and help us through hard times if we seek Him and rest in Him. It doesn't mean we won't feel anxious and wonder what God is doing, but we will know He is in control.

"Trust in the Lord with all your heart and lean not on your own understanding; in all your ways submit to him, and he will make your paths straight" (Proverbs 3:5-6). Trust God's best for your family. Lean on Him and do not trust others' understanding, or even your own, unless it is grounded in the firm foundation of Scripture. Sometimes we can look too much to respected individuals' advice. We might even look to good Christian books when we want to change a habit or enhance something in our lives. These can be helpful, but they don't take into account our uniqueness.

As women of God, we have unique struggles, passions, interests, and gifts we can learn from and share with our children. Enjoy what God has given you and seek Him in your struggles. Trust that He has put you on this path. Trust that what He is teaching you is for you and your family.

Go Deeper:

Do you have areas of your life, even small areas, in which you have not asked God for guidance? Make a list right now of the struggles in your life, or the things you would like to change. Pray over that list and give it to God. He cares about each choice we make (1 Peter 5:7). Let Him guide you and lead you. Then, rest in Him and continue to seek Him daily to stay on the path.

What's Next?

Enjoy your children! Stop looking to the right or the left, wondering if you are doing everything right! Explore your passions with them and help them find their own. Seek the Lord for their correct path. Then, patiently guide them to His will for their futures. Rest in the Lord and His plan for you and your family. Smile at the future as the woman in Psalm 31 does!

Further Study:

- Jeremiah 29:11-14   • Proverbs 4:20-27   • Isaiah 30:20-21   • Proverbs 3:1-12

journal

_____

_____

_____

_____

_____

_____

_____

_____

_____

_____

_____

_____

_____

_____

_____

_____

_____

_____

_____

> "'For I know the plans I have for you,' declares the LORD,
> 'plans to prosper you and not to harm you,
> plans to give you hope and a future.'"
>
> ~ Jeremiah 29:11

God has Big Plans for You!

By: Tara Davis

Do you feel like your life is too messy to be used by God? Is your marriage, child, thought life, anxiety, depression, disorganization, or insecurity too difficult a puzzle? Maybe, if you get your life together first, God could find some beautiful purpose for you?

Sweet mama, those are lies from the enemy, spoken to you with the intent of making you ineffective for God (John 8:44). Jesus is bigger than your problems, and He wants to use you amid your struggles to bring Him glory (I John 4:4b). In fact, God often uses our hurts and failings to produce His greatest work in us (Isaiah 61:3)!

I have to be honest, I'm right there with you, my friend. Life tends to be hard. I never guessed that the Lord would allow me to serve and disciple three incredible sons. Furthermore, not even in my wildest dreams did I imagine that He would have me here with Help Club for Moms writing these letters to you!

Believe that God has a ministry for you too, regardless of where you are in your life and in your walk with the Lord (1 Peter 4:10). Ministry does not just take place in a church or Bible study, however. Ministry is the everyday loving, serving, and encouraging of those around you. Soften yourself to the voice of the Holy Spirit. Is He asking you to talk to someone who is lonely, bring a meal to someone who is sick, or encourage another mama in a challenging season with little ones?

The Lord wants to use you right now, right where you are (Philippians 2:13). However, make no mistake; He will use your ministry to others to minister to you! He will not leave you where you are but will work in your heart to make you more like Him. As you serve and encourage those around you, He will grow you spiritually. He will heal your heart as He uses you to heal others. While you lean on God to fill in your places of inadequacy, He will teach you who He is and who you are in Him. As you see to meeting the needs of hurting people, He will meet your needs in ways you will never comprehend! Do not wait; the time to seek God's purposes for you is at hand! Trust Him to use you where you are now and to eternally change you during the process.

Go Deeper:

Stop putting off your ministry until "someday" and start praying that God will show you ways in which He wants to use you now. Pray that God will give you wisdom and open your eyes to His purposes for this time in your life. Journal any promptings of the Holy Spirit that come to your mind and lay them back down before the Lord.

What's Next?

Regardless of whatever else God has planned for you, your family is your first and most important ministry! Without a doubt, God is calling you to love and serve your husband and children. You are

Week Six ~ Day Three

Week Six

the best one to share the good news and love of Jesus with your children daily, and you are your husband's primary source of affection and encouragement. The difference you can make in the lives of those closest to you is astronomical!

Journal

_____

_____

_____

_____

_____

_____

_____

_____

_____

_____

_____

_____

_____

_____

_____

_____

_____

_____

_____

_____

"And this is the testimony:
God has given us eternal life and this life is in His Son."
~ 1 John 5:11

The Power of our Testimony

By: Rae-Ellen Sanders

Praise God, He has called each of us to the saving knowledge of Jesus Christ! Have you ever wondered where your life would be now if you didn't ask Jesus into your heart? What paths would you have chosen to walk down? As Christians, we have had the most remarkable transformation happen in our lives when the blood of Jesus washed us clean. What an exciting privilege we now have to tell others our salvation story.

Recently, in my small group, I shared my testimony. It had been a while since I told anyone how the Lord grabbed a hold of my heart and turned my life around. I was anxious to expose my personal history, even in front of loving friends. I had made bad decisions and my previous worldly sin made me embarrassed and nervous. What I realized is that my friends were scared too. With God's help, the eight of us shared our stories that day. We were all astonished at how unique our lives and experiences were, and how God reached down from heaven to save us with His amazing grace!

A paradigm shift happens in our soul when we have a life-changing encounter with the Lord. We should be so joy-filled and in awe that Jesus forgave our sin, that we share the Good News with everyone we meet! Broadcasting what Jesus has radically done in our lives is worth getting excited about! So why don't we do it at every opportunity? Many will agree that it is NOT easy! It takes time and courage to review our lives and openly share our transformation with others. The enemy of our souls also wants to keep us chained in shame. Be encouraged, moms, that 1 Corinthians 2:4-5 will exhort you to trust in the Lord's power when stepping out in faith!

When we act in obedience, we will not only glorify God and influence others, but we will also allow our testimonies to become great examples for our children. Speaking about our past compared to our lives lived in victory will illustrate God's work within us and instruct our children in the way they should go (Proverbs 22:6)! Ultimately, God uses our conversion story to help others put their trust in Him.

1 Corinthians 1:26-31:

> Brothers and sisters, think of what you were when you were called. Not many of you were wise by human standards; not many were influential; not many were of noble birth. But God chose the foolish things of the world to shame the wise; God chose the weak things of the world to shame the strong. God chose the lowly things of this world and the despised things—and the things that are not—to nullify the things that are, so that no one may boast before him. It is because of him that you are in Christ Jesus, who has become for us wisdom from God—that is, our righteousness, holiness, and redemption. Therefore, as it is written: "Let the one who boasts boast in the Lord."

Go Deeper:

Have you ever shared your testimony with others? If you haven't, or if it's been a while, take some time to ask the Lord to refresh your memory. You can start by writing down a few sentences about what you were like before you made a decision to follow Jesus Christ. Then remember how you came to believe in Jesus and how your life has changed since. It should only take three minutes to tell the story of how you came to trust in Jesus.

What's Next?

Salvation creates a transformation in us. When we tell of what God has done, we gain boldness that will propel us to share the Gospel more. The more we talk about Jesus at home, the easier it is to talk about Him with others. Look for opportunities to share the love of Jesus by sharing your testimony and encouraging your children to share Jesus with their friends too!

Journal

_____
_____
_____
_____
_____
_____
_____
_____
_____
_____
_____
_____
_____
_____
_____
_____
_____
_____

Food for the Soul

Zucchini is one of the easiest and most prolific vegetables to grow. When you plant a zucchini seed in nutrient-rich soil it will sprout and grow into a flowering bush. As long as the birds do not devour it, it will yield more zucchini than you, your family and your friends know what to do with! Were you to count all the seeds that one zucchini plant produces, you would find it yields over a hundredfold.

In Luke 8, Jesus tells the parable of the sower:

> A sower went out to sow his seed. And as he sowed, some fell along the path and was trampled underfoot, and the birds of the air devoured it. And some fell on the rock, and as it grew up, it withered away, because it had no moisture. And some fell among thorns, and the thorns grew up with it and choked it. And some fell into good soil and grew and yielded a hundredfold. (Luke 8:5-8)

Jesus explains that the seed is the Word of God and as we read it, it is being sown into our hearts. Once there it will take root if we water it daily. Reading the Word once and then forgetting what you read is like the seed that fell on the rocks. And the seed grown up in doubt and unbelief is like the seed choked by the thorns. What kind of seed are you growing in your heart? What will happen to it? Will the enemy steal it? Will the weeds of the culture choke it out? We want our hearts to be like good soil. We want to be "those, who after hearing the word, hold it fast in an honest and good heart, and bear fruit with patience" (Luke 8:15).

My grandma, who went to be with Jesus when I was five years old, left us a delicious chocolate zucchini cake recipe to remember her by. As you bake it and enjoy it, think of the parable of the sower! Pray that you will hear the Word of God, hold it in your heart and that you will bear much fruit, fruit that will last! I hope you are blessed by your own or someone's abundant zucchini harvest this summer.

CHOCOLATE ZUCCHINI CAKE   By: Jennifer Valdois

Ingredients

- 2 ½ cups flour
- ½ cup cocoa
- 2 ½ tsp. baking powder
- 1 ½ tsp. baking soda
- 1 tsp. salt
- 1 tsp. cinnamon
- ¾ cup butter
- 2 cups sugar
- 3 eggs
- 2 tsp. vanilla
- 2 cups coarsely shredded zucchini
- ½ cup milk
- 1 cup chopped nuts, optional
- Powdered sugar

Directions:

1. Combine the flour, cocoa, baking powder, baking soda, salt, and cinnamon. Set aside.
2. In a different mixing bowl, beat together the butter and sugar, add the eggs, and beat well. Stir in the dry ingredients and the milk. Add the nuts, if using.
3. Bake in a well-oiled bundt pan or loaf pan at 350 degrees for one hour, or until done.
4. Cool 15 minutes, then remove from pan. Sprinkle with powdered sugar.

Summer of Joy

~ Week Seven ~

Hello Friend,

These golden days of summer are so beautiful as your children desperately soak up the last rays of warm sun on their skin, the cool evenings playing outside until the sun sets, and each free minute doing the things they love most. But even beautiful things can stretch long and wear a mama clean out. Are you there yet? Are you ready for a little time off from the long loveliness of summer?

I feel as if I am daily needing a reminder that this time with my kids is so precious. They are only young once. The continual stream of pillow forts, mud tracked into the house, sticky fingerprints on the windows, and perpetual requests for snacks will quickly pass before these boys of mine will stand taller than I and won't need me in the same way they do now.

I want to finish well. I want to finish this summer in a way that will bring glory to my Savior. How can I wake up to God's calling on my life in these last days of sunshine and freedom before the school year begins again in earnest? How can I walk through these days with love, joy, peace, patience, kindness, goodness, faithfulness, gentleness and self-control (Galatians 5:22-23)?

I can wake up each day, ready to live for Jesus as a mom! I can lovingly make special plans that I have put off all summer and take joy in spending time playing with my boys. I can pray aloud with them during moments of conflict, that God will give them (and me) a spirit of peace. I can use patience when dealing with the messes and kindness in my words to my children. I can show them a picture of goodness in the decisions I make and faithfulness as I spend daily time with the Lord. I can respond with gentleness and self-control when I am frustrated. I can serve the Lord in these days with my children.

And if I can do it, sister, you can do it too, because with God's strength all things are possible (Philippians 4:13). He is carrying you through these last days of summer with your children. How will you choose to finish well?

So much love to you!

Tara Davis and the Help Club For Moms Team

> *Whatever you do in word or deed, do all in the name of the Lord Jesus, giving thanks through Him to God the Father.*
>
> *~ Colossians 3:17*

Mom Tips

By: Leslie Leonard

The wise woman builds her house.
~ Proverbs 14:1a

The Wise Woman Builds Her Spirit

Every morning this week, challenge yourself by not turning on your phone until you have spent 15 minutes in the presence of God. Use the time to pray and read your Bible.

The Wise Woman Loves Her Husband

Journal about what you appreciate most about your husband this week. If you feel led, share with your husband what you wrote about him.

The Wise Woman Loves Her Children

Ask your children to identify a classmate from the school year who was often left out during recess time. Invite the child (and his or her mom) over for the afternoon to play and have popsicles. Use this activity to remind your children to show the love of Jesus through their actions.

The Wise Woman Cares For Her Home

Take time this week to organize underneath the sinks and inside the drawers in your bathrooms. Throw away any expired or empty items. Fully wipe out all areas and place like items together. Also, know what's for dinner by 9 AM each day this week.

"Satisfy us in the morning with your unfailing love
that we will sing for joy and be glad all of our days."

~ Psalm 90:14

Keeper of the Chocolate

By: Heather Doolittle

While contemplating the wide-eyed wonder and belly laughs of childhood, I realized I hold a very important position as a mother: the keeper of the chocolate, the planner of parties, and basically the facilitator of joy. It seems unfair that I hold this power in my family. I know that if any of my children had this right, they would exercise it freely—sweets and roller coasters for everyone!

When the Bible tells us women will be saved through childbirth, does that saving grace come in part through the rose-colored glasses with which children show us the world (1 Timothy 2:15)? God is exponentially better, His love immensely greater than we could possibly fathom, and small children seem to inherently get it.

However, I've often missed small opportunities for laughter and fun in a quest for order and efficiency. How many times have I singled-handedly squelched my children's joy? Denied a dip in the stream to avoid scrubbing mud from their clothes, refused a chance to paint a masterpiece to prevent paint-covered fingers and walls. There is a time and place for everything; I am certainly not suggesting you live as a slave to every whim of your child. It's all about finding the proper balance.

I resolve to become more like a child, as Jesus instructed His disciples—to laugh and love with abandon, leaving my cares to my Heavenly Father. Isn't that how God intends for us to live? Surely He derives pleasure from witnessing His children delight in small gifts, just as we do with our little ones.

God has given us this awesome world in which to live, and I intend to bask in the beauty of it. I pray He will open my eyes as I study my children, and help me to see all that is beautiful and precious—that He will teach me to immerse myself in pure, exuberant joy as I learn to live and love as God's holy and dearly-loved child (Colossians 3:12). I want to take my family alongside me as I bask in God's abundant love, goodness, beauty, and grace every day and emanate sincere, abundant joy all my life (Psalm 90:14).

Go Deeper:

Are there ways in which you should learn to become like a child? For example, do you yell at your children to clean their rooms when you ought to turn on some music, dance, and clean a bit less efficiently? (I'm guilty of this)

Pray that you may relish in God's blessings, internalize them, and let His joy and peace flow through you.

What's Next?

Resolve to see the world through the delighted eyes of your sweet children instead of forcing them to see our tiresome, grown-up world. Look for the simple blessings in your life. Give thanks aloud and rejoice; ask your children to do the same.

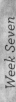
Plan a special way to bless your family—an evening trip to the park, a favorite meal by candlelight, or a heartfelt love note. Revel in the joy of your loved ones. Read Psalm 90:14, and remind them of your quest for joy that starts with Jesus' love!

journal

_____

_____

_____

_____

_____

_____

_____

_____

_____

_____

_____

_____

_____

_____

_____

_____

_____

_____

_____

_____

_____

_____

_____

"Make a joyful shout to the Lord, all you lands! Serve the Lord
with gladness; Come before His presence with singing.
Know that the Lord, He is God; It is He who has made us, not
we ourselves; We are His people and the sheep of His pasture."

~ Psalm 100:1-3 (NKJV)

Choosing Joy

By: Leslie Leonard

This morning I had a conversation with my six-year-old daughter about the characteristics of God. I asked Ruby to tell me about God and how He makes her feel inside her heart. Her answers brought a smile to my face. According to my sweet girl, God is loving and joyful.

Will you join me in choosing joy this summer? Let's look at the world through the eyes of a hopeful, six-year-old girl who has nothing but love to give. Here are some helpful and practical tips that will help you choose joy:

- **Joy comes when we spend time in God's presence:** Psalm 28:7 (ESV) tells us, "The Lord is my strength and my shield. I trust Him with all my heart. He helps me, and my heart is filled with joy. I burst out in songs of thanksgiving."

- **Joy is not dependent on your circumstances:** Psalm 27:5-6 (ESV) tells us, "For he will conceal me there when troubles come; he will hide me in his sanctuary. He will place me out of reach on a high rock. Then I will hold my head high above my enemies who surround me. At his sanctuary I will offer sacrifices with shouts of joy, singing and praising the Lord with music."

- **Joy comes when we spend our lives praising God:** Psalm 47:1-3 (ESV) says, "Come, everyone! Clap your hands! Shout to God with joyful praise! For the Lord Most High is awesome. He is the great King of all the earth. He subdues the nations before us, putting our enemies beneath our feet."

- **Joy fills you up when you feel empty on the inside:** Romans 15:13 (ESV) says, "I pray that God, the source of hope, will fill you completely with joy and peace because you trust in him. Then you will overflow with confident hope through the power of the Holy Spirit."

- **Joy is not an emotion that can be fake or forced:** Isaiah 35:10 (ESV) tells us, "Those who have been ransomed by the Lord will return. They will enter Jerusalem singing, crowned with everlasting joy. Sorrow and mourning will disappear, and they will be filled with joy and gladness."

Go Deeper:

How can you live out God's love and joy today? Write these ideas in your journal.

What's Next?

Grab your children, a bunch of pots and pans, and some spatulas and wooden spoons. We are going to put Psalm 100 into action. Let's make some joyful noise unto the Lord! Tell your children to be as loud as possible. Encourage them to try to reach Heaven with their voices. Let them be noisy. Let go of all that control and just be present in that moment with your children. Take a photo of your family band and share it on the Help Club For Moms Facebook page.

journal

"Give thanks in all circumstances;
for this is God's will for you in Christ Jesus."

~ 1 Thessalonians 5:18

"Those who sacrifice thank offerings honor me,
and to the blameless I will show my salvation."

~ Psalm 50:23

An Attitude of Gratitude

By: Rae-Ellen Sanders

Many of the studies I've read over this summer have been amazing exhortations to us as women to not compare ourselves with others or degrade our abilities as mothers. I completely agree! Moms, our work as mothers is unique to our individual children and circumstances, and is so important! The enemy of our soul truly uses these pits of comparison, doubt, and fatigue to make us feel inferior and, quite frankly, like failures. Don't listen to Satan's lies! Even if we've made mistakes, Jesus wants to wash us with grace and equip us with what we need daily to parent our crew well!

Don't get me wrong, life can be hard. It is so easy to be ungrateful in our situations and to be under the illusion that we can't find joy amidst trials and heartache! Struggles are real, but when we give thanks to the Lover of our souls, Jesus replaces those thoughts and feeling with hope and joy.

The action of giving thanks changes our perspective. Daily household duties, debt, and the drama of life can be overwhelming and leave us in despair. However, going about our days with a purpose to find something to be thankful for will cause transformation in our lives! Perhaps our burden won't disappear, but our approach to those burdens will change. When you give thanks to God, you will receive the peace of God!

Philippians 4:6-7:
> Do not be anxious about anything, but in every situation, by prayer and petition, with thanksgiving, present your requests to God. And the peace of God, which transcends all understanding, will guard your hearts and your minds in Christ Jesus.

New York Times Best Seller author Ann Voskamp counts her blessings in a very poetic book called *1,000 Gifts*. Challenged to find 1,000 ways of being thankful, she composed a daily journal, and encourages us to do the same. I've read this book, and this concept of gratitude has changed my life. Finding something grand, like the sunset, or something minute like shade on a hot summer day, and having a heart of gratitude, will deepen our relationship with the Lord. The benefit of writing down what you are grateful for re-emphasizes God's goodness. It also allows you to look back on days past with an appreciation of God's faithfulness.

We need to get into a habit of being thankful in both good times and bad (Colossians 3:17). Whispering a prayer of gratitude invites God to work in our lives and gives us fresh insight into our circumstances. You can easily say, "Thank you Holy Spirit for filling me with peace when I feel so unraveled. Show me how to be content with what you give me and help me to see your hand at work." Simply being appreciative of a dishwasher or a washing machine has helped me go about my chores of doing laundry for a family of seven with a better approach. When we start to count all things as joy, and praise the Lord for big and little things, our attitude will be one of gratitude.

Week Seven ~ Day Three

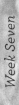

Go Deeper:

Have you taken time in your day to list the things you are grateful for? Why not read Ann Voskamp's *1,000 Gifts* and start your own journal of thanksgiving? It might be a challenge to you at first, but the more you look around you for things to appreciate and value, your list will grow. You might even need more than one journal!

What's Next?

You can take Gratitude a step further by teaching your kids to be thankful too. Encourage them to keep a journal as well. Cultivating an attitude of gratitude in your family will help them be more altruistic and positive. Studies show they will be more attentive, get better grades, and have more determination if they practice this attitude. This lesson is better caught than taught; so let your kids see you being thankful by praising the Lord not only with your words but also with your deeds.

journal

_____

_____

_____

_____

_____

_____

_____

_____

_____

_____

_____

_____

_____

_____

_____

_____

"Now all glory to God, who is able,
through his mighty power at work within us,
to accomplish infinitely more than we might ask or think."

~ Ephesians 3:20 (NLT)

Dare to Dream

By: Meagan Witt

I used to pride myself on being a realist, someone who wouldn't dare spend valuable time dreaming. However, that was life before Jesus, and of course, our Savior is much too kind to allow us to live a life without dreams.

In fact, sweet mama, did you know that Jesus Himself put those dreams deep inside your heart? You know, the dreams you wouldn't dare say out loud, the ones you brush to the side and say to yourself..."impossible." Luke 1:37 tell us, "For nothing is impossible with God."

In Jeremiah 29:11 God tells us, "'For I know the plans I have for you' declares the Lord 'Plans to prosper you and not to harm you, plans to give you hope and a future.'" He is telling us that *nothing* is impossible with Almighty God and reminding us that His plans for us are good and infinitely beyond our highest prayers, desires, thoughts, and hopes.

You see, those big dreams we have, He gave them to us. I like to call them "God dreams" because they are dreams so big that if God isn't in them, we will fail. That's how we know they are from Him. Rick Warren, author of *The Purpose Driven Life*, says,

> The first thing God does to build your faith is to give you a dream. When God wants to work in your life, He'll always give you a dream—about yourself, about what He wants you to do, about how He's going to use your life to impact the world.

If we look to God's Word, we see Him giving His people dreams to stretch their faith again and again. God gave Noah the dream of building an ark, Joseph the dream of being a leader who would save his people, and Abraham the dream of being the father of a great nation. That is just to name a few. God uses dreams.

I once heard Christine Caine say that, "Life is too short, the world is too big, and God's love is too great to live an ordinary life." Sisters, know this. Believe this. How different might our world look if we as women of God stepped out in bold faith, believing that the One who gave us these beautiful, scary, big "God dreams" would be faithful to complete them? And what if the generation behind us saw their mamas doing just that? After all, Meg Meeker says that "the most powerful way to teach a daughter how to enjoy her life and find her true purpose is to let her see her mother do the same."

Go Deeper:

Spend time in prayer, search your heart, and ask God to show you the dreams He has for you and your family.

What's Next?

Believe, sweet mama. Grab hold of these dreams and don't let anything or anyone shake them from you. Remember, they are from your Father. Keep in mind the children in your home who are watching you. Step out in bold faith, and ask God daily what the next step will be toward your dreams.

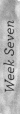
Jesus replied, "What do you mean, 'If I can?'...anything is possible if a person believes" (Mark 9:23 NLT).

Know This: All of us at the Help Club for Moms are believing with you. We are asking God to stir up "God dreams" in His daughters. We believe He will not only stir up dreams, but He will also be faithful to bring them to fruition.

"The one who calls you is faithful, and He will do it" (1 Thessalonians 5:24).

Journal

_____

_____

_____

_____

_____

_____

_____

_____

_____

_____

_____

_____

_____

_____

_____

_____

_____

_____

_____

_____

Giving Your Kids the *Gift* of *Wonder!*

By: Tara Davis

"The heavens declare the glory of God, the skies proclaim the work of His hands."
– Psalm 19:1

God has created this magnificent world as a love-gift to us! How can we instill wonder at God's creation within the hearts of our children?

Here are some ideas for you!

1. **Get outdoors every day with your children!**
   Whether it is for a walk around your yard or to hike a trail, spend time together exploring God's creation.

2. **Start a nature collection.**
   Designate a space—possibly a bucket, box, or table—for your children to place all of the interesting rocks and leaves they pick up outside. Cheap magnifying glasses make observing these new discoveries even more interesting!

3. **Have your child keep a nature journal.**
   Use a notebook or sketch pad to draw or write about the beautiful things they observe in nature.

4. **Notice the small beauties in God's creation.**
   An intricate leaf, drop of dew, or colorful sunset are all conversation starters to introduce your children to the concept of noticing the fingerprints of God all throughout our natural world.

5. **Together with your children, thank God for His amazing creation.**
   As you notice little blessings in the world around you, be sure to praise God out loud for those gifts!

Summer of Joy

~ Week Eight ~

Dear Sister,

Isn't summer one of the most beautiful times of the year? I love how everything is growing and green and in full bloom. I'm a mom of teenagers now and I can't help but notice the similarity in them. They have entered an exciting time in life. They are growing up and their future is bright with hopes and dreams.

But, for me, the countdown has begun. I only have a limited time with them in my home and under my wing. While they are excited about what lies ahead, I can get sad, knowing the years will go by so quickly.

As this summer approached, I prayed about what I could do to make the most of my time with my teenagers. I don't want to get so busy, filling each day with activities and my to-do list, that I don't take time to invest in them. Now that they are self-sufficient, it's easy to let them do their own thing, and at the same time, they are not as excited as they used to be about my ideas! I need to think of new ways to reach into their world and touch their hearts. I brainstormed about meaningful ways to connect and I encourage you to do the same. No matter how long the days may seem, the years are short. Before we know it, our children will be ready to take flight. While I am not eager for that day to come, the God of hope has been teaching me that if I invest in them and our relationship now, while they are young, then their leaving home will not be the end, but a new beginning of a lifelong friendship.

This week we share some studies geared toward parenting older children. Whether you have teenagers or littles, I encourage you to pray for your relationship with your children to grow deeper with each passing year, starting this summer.

Love and Blessings,

Jennifer Valdois and the Help Club for Moms Team

> *Let us not become weary in doing good,*
> *for at the proper time we will reap a harvest if we do not give up.*
> *~ Galatians 6:9*

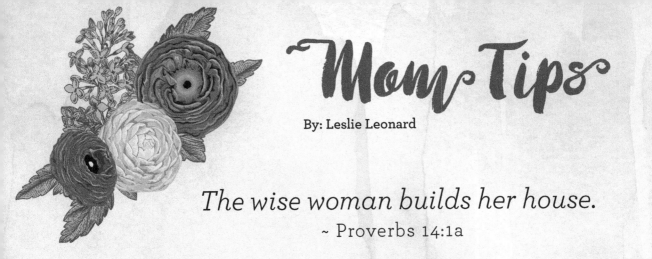

Mom Tips

By: Leslie Leonard

The wise woman builds her house.
~ Proverbs 14:1a

The Wise Woman Builds Her Spirit

Write Isaiah 41:10 in your journal, on your mirror, or on a note card. Memorize the verse by the end of the week. Pray the Scripture over your family.

The Wise Woman Loves Her Husband

Show that you are happy to see your husband when he comes home from work for the day. Be sure to smile when he enters the home, and give him a hug and/or a kiss! Let him know by your actions that he is loved.

The Wise Woman Loves Her Children

Every morning this week, wake up in the morning *for* your children instead of *to* your children. There is a difference. Set your alarm to get up before your kids, and then smile and tell them you are happy to see them when they wake up.

The Wise Woman Cares For Her Home

Utilize the Weekly Plan Sheet and take 20 minutes Sunday afternoon to plan your week, strategize, and set yourself up for success. You can find this at our website www.HelpClubForMoms.com in the sidebar on the left under "Plan Your Week!" Also, Take a few "15 Minute Cleaning Sprints" this week. Set a timer and work as fast as you can in one area of your house. Vacuum, dust, or clean a bathroom. You will be surprised how much you can get done in 15 minutes!

> "For we do not have a high priest who is unable to empathize with our weaknesses, but we have one who has been tempted in every way, just as we are—yet He did not sin."
> ~ Hebrews 4:15

Identifying With Jesus

By: Mari Jo Mast

"In the day-to-day experience of life, we have opportunities to learn to be like Jesus, to choose to be patient, to be considerate, to help others, to pray. On the job and in our homes, Jesus has something to say about what we do." – Michael Morrison

One revolutionary truth stands out to me about Jesus: He identifies with us.

John 1:14 explains: "He became flesh and dwelt among us." In Philippians 2:6-8, we learn Jesus humbly obeyed the Father, He left all the glory of Heaven and came down to the earth and took on the nature of a servant. Although He was God, he appeared in human likeness. Hebrews 4:15 says He was tempted in every way just like we are.

This astounds and comforts me. It shows God's secure identity, His love for us, His practicality, His interest in mere humanity. It also proves His relevance to our everyday activities and struggles. Because Jesus understands and knows our weakness, He identifies with us.

But can we identify with Him?

I remember a few years ago, I ignorantly questioned Jesus: *How can you understand what it's like to be a mother if you never had any children?* I was sitting on the porch on a hot summer day; my head leaned back on a soft, cushioned chair. I felt utterly hopeless because of an argument I was having with one of my teens. I had spoken harshly out of anger, and my heart grieved. I wallowed in defeat and didn't think Jesus could identify with me as a mom. So how could He help? His answer took me by surprise: *I had twelve, and one betrayed me.* I cannot say how deeply the words broke through my discouragement, yet what He spoke next ministered even more to my broken heart: *Don't take it personally when your children choose not to obey or love you. Although Judas was with me every day and saw my heart, He still chose to do His own thing. I didn't stop him.*

As these words softly made their way into my heart, I knew Jesus understood and identified profoundly more than I had given him credit! He also revealed something else to me within the same breath: When I parent His way instead of mine, I cannot be offended. Will I identify with Him?

I guess I never thought about the fact that Judas' heart had been revealed to Jesus long before the night he was betrayed. He saw him stealing the coins from the money bag, saw the disdain on his face when the prostitute poured costly ointment on His feet. Not only did Jesus see Judas' actions, He saw his murderous heart too; He could read his mind and thoughts. Never once did He try to stop Him. He taught and parented the twelve from a place of security because He listened to the Father.

Offense and condemnation come as a result of parenting our own way, in our own strength. As a mother, it's easy to parent from this place, to feel hurt when a child disobeys or refuses to surrender. We try to force or manipulate her or him to think our way. Becoming offended causes us to condemn rather than love.

~ 99 ~

Week Eight ~ Day One

That day, though I had parented my way, I never once felt condemned, only deeply understood, deeply loved, and deeply dipped in grace. Jesus didn't condemn Judas, and He didn't condemn me. He wasn't offended and identified with me.

Mom, Jesus understands and doesn't condemn you either. He's not offended because He listens to the Father.

Jesus only did what He saw His Father do. If He didn't take it personally, we shouldn't either. If He didn't force or manipulate Judas to surrender to Him as King of Heaven but instead continued to love and serve him to His own death, then why should we parent any differently?

He teaches and parents better than offense and condemnation.

When we identify with Jesus in our parenting, the outcome ultimately belongs to the Lord. We leave the results to Him.

As Jesus prayed and humbly obeyed the Father, so we should pray and humbly obey Jesus in our mothering. The key to identifying with Jesus comes from laying down our lives like He did, our own "rights," and our expectations—by living and loving our children as He loves all His children.

This is how we identify with Him.

Go Deeper:

Do you truly believe Jesus became human? Why or why not? Look up John 1:14, 18 and Hebrews 2:16-18. Do you believe Jesus identifies with your struggles as a mom? Write your thoughts and musings in your journal.

What's Next?

Pray with me: "*Dear Jesus, I desire more than anything else to identify with you. As you listened and obeyed the Father, so I want to hear and obey you. Open my spiritual eyes and ears to see and hear what you are doing and saying. Help me selflessly lay down my life as you laid down yours. Please help me receive your love so I can love my children well. I choose to lay down my "rights" and my expectations as a mom to follow your lead. I know you care deeply and will help me. Amen.*"

Journal

_____

_____

_____

_____

_____

_____

_____

_____

"See, darkness covers the earth and thick darkness
is over the peoples, but the LORD rises upon you
and his glory appears over you."

~ Isaiah 60:2

A Letter to My Teens About Dating

By: Kara Schrock

Dear Children,

In a world where family, marriage, and genders are on trial, you need to know that our future generations are at stake.

If Hollywood is setting the standard, you can be assured that *50 Shades of Gray* and *The Bachelorette* are ruling your dad and me outdated and your grandparents old-fashioned and boring. What are you looking to as a role model? Is it the new release down the street? Or is it the generation of honor and respect that kept your grandparents in love for 40 years? Yes, ol' fashioned is unpopular, but you know what? Sometimes it's ok to rebel against the popular. Here's to a good start:

Sons:

- If you fall in love with a girl's face, your love will fade with her beauty.
- If you fall in love with her soul, your love will grow deeper with age.
- She needs to know you have eyes for her alone and that she is more valuable to you than any other!
- The right one will bring out your best. She will nurture your talents, encourage your exploits, and talk good ol' common sense when you need it most!

Daughters:

- You should know that a man's heart is more tender and loyal than you might think.
- Treat him like a king, and he will give you the kingdom! He wants to spoil you: carry your bags, open doors, and pick up the tab. Let him. This is a good sign that he will help you with dirty dishes and a messy house if you marry him. He will want to take risks and be brave. Support him because you trust him!
- Don't play with his heart by cuddling, kissing, and crying to get your way. This breaks trust and creates disrespect.
- The right man for you will bring out your best! He will lead you spiritually, allow you to pursue your dreams, and hear your heart. Hang on to him.

Children:

- Passion is good and of God, don't bury it. Instead, cultivate it and direct it in righteousness.
- Physical attraction to the opposite sex is normal, natural, and good! Don't feel guilt or condemnation for a healthy appreciation of beauty or strength. God is an amazing artist and knows how to give good gifts! However, if you feed your natural tendencies with pornography or uncontrolled thoughts of lust, this is where you will derail. The wreckage will cost you more than you want to pay. It's not worth it!
- You should not expect sex from your dating partner, nor should you even think to ask for it!

- You have what it takes to turn the tide! You can bring back chivalry and honor and enjoy a long, satisfying, and adventurous life!

Love,
Your Forever Mom

Go Deeper:

So often, we parent out of fear or past regret. Release these mistakes to God and trust Him to do immeasurably more than all you ask or imagine, according to his power that is at work within you and your children (Ephesians 3:20).

What's Next?

Write a letter to your teenagers and lay it on their bed, sealed with a kiss (if you like this letter, write it out in your own handwriting and sign your name). If you are looking for more resources on dating in today's world, I highly recommend the book, *Courtship In Crisis* by Tomas Umstattd Jr.

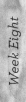

Journal

_____

_____

_____

_____

_____

_____

_____

_____

_____

_____

_____

_____

_____

_____

_____

_____

_____

_____

> "For as he thinks in his heart, so is he..."
>
> ~ Proverbs 23:7a (NKJV)

> "Above all else, guard your heart,
> for everything you do flows from it."
>
> ~ Proverbs 4:23

Addressing Gender Questions with Faith

By: Christie Frieg

All through my early years, I wanted to be a boy. I never played with dolls, wore skirts, or liked the girly-girls. I traipsed through the woods with my grandpa, hunting for mushrooms, lizards, and adventure. Dragons fascinated me—I would rarely be caught without some sort of tail pinned onto my pants or wings attached to my back. Even with the few girlfriends I had, our games of choice involved secret agents, explorers, or warring empires. Today, I have a second-degree black belt, high scores in shoot-'em-up games, a love for science fiction and rock music, and a degree in computer science. What would culture say to that?

Most likely, the gender experts of our day would recommend that I be "transitioned" from a girl to a boy. After all, I clearly should have been born one—in fact, if you had asked me from age 4-10 if I wanted to be a boy, I probably would have said yes! But luckily for me, in my early years, such a question never crossed anyone's mind. And today, happily married to my husband, I glory in my femininity.

But alas, the children of this day face confusion, a struggle with issues that should never even enter our minds as a viable possibility. I believe we lost this battle as soon as we accepted the idea that people could be born the wrong gender. As we opened this door, we started looking at gender situations much differently.

We watch 7-year-old Christie, stomping around the yard with wings and a tail claiming to be the dragon named "King Ghidora," and instead of seeing her as an imaginative girl playing a game, we now see her as a gender-confused girl stuck in the wrong body. The innocent game of pretend suddenly carries heavy significance. The parents' hushed conversations, overheard by the little girl, strike her with confusion and anxiety. Thoughts that should never be taken seriously now haunt her through her already-confusing teen years. And thus, we have the gender crisis we face today.

Moms, if you have a child who fits the description I gave of my younger self, fear not. Whatever you do, do not listen to the demonic voices of culture as they plant seeds of doubt in your heart. Your child is normal. Little boys don't have to play superheroes—they can do crafts and play house instead. Little girls don't need dolls or makeup or dresses to be secure in their femininity. The greatest gift you can give them is acceptance and protection from the insidious lies about what their likes and dislikes supposedly mean.

Go Deeper:

Even if your child doesn't fit the mold I've described here, I'm sure you can think of a place in your parenting where you struggle trusting God. Pray and ask God to show you these areas and write them in your journal. Then write down five of your child's strengths and pray for God to help you encourage these qualities in your child.

What's Next?

Remember that your words to your children carry incredible power—they will internalize the words you speak over them, and they will pick up on any doubting or fearful undertones. This week, set a reminder on your phone to help you remember to intentionally speak life to your child. Ask God to give you the right words to help you speak words of faith, and prophesy truth and godliness over them.

Some examples might be: "I'm so thankful God gave me a daughter like you!" or "God is making you into a man of strength and integrity!"

Shut out the voices and press on in faith and joy—this is the greatest gift you can give your child.

Journal

> "Why, you do not even know what will happen tomorrow.
> What is your life? You are a mist that appears
> for a little while and then vanishes."
>
> ~ James 4:14

No Do-Overs

By: Kristi Valentine

In our family, when one of our children acts unkindly, we ask if that child would like a "do-over." It's a moment of parental grace in which the child rethinks the mistake and has a second chance to respond with respect and love. Everyone's heart is healed, and everyone feels loved. As parents, we love this moment that is chock-full of discipleship and grace!

Wouldn't it be wonderful if real life had do-overs? Imagine you're too busy to make good eye contact while your child shares her feelings? Or, perhaps you're too tired to mentally engage in that time of play? If only we could just take a do-over! Unfortunately, more often than not, the moment passes and we heartbreakingly realize we missed the opportunity to show love.

Psalm 144:4 says, "our days are like a fleeting shadow," and James 4:14 says, "our life is but a mist that appears for a little while and vanishes." My call to all you beautiful mamas is this: life is short, so love your children well today. Frankly, this is also a call to myself. Tears well up in my eyes as countless scenes of our family's daily life flash through my mind: half-listening, on the phone too much, over-scheduled, mixed-up priorities.

More tears come as I recollect, in contrast, the constant whisper of the Holy Spirit to me saying, "Love them well." Not kidding here: God tells me to love my children well nearly every day.

He is a good Father, and He gently nudges me so lovingly. So no "mama guilt" allowed while reading this! The best response is a simple acknowledgment deep in the heart that improvements are needed, along with a genuine, giant step toward God.

Does it sound impossible to change things in your home? Romans 7:18b says, "I have the desire to do what is good, but I cannot carry it out." We all feel this way at times, but be relieved because God will do it all through you. Have a soft heart to authentically and deeply pursue God so He can teach you the art of loving your children well.

Go Deeper:

Test your heart. Are you living by your own thoughts and desires or by the Holy Spirit's? Love is a fruit of the Holy Spirit in your life. Invite Him to lead and guide you as you love your children well.

Remember that God's grace can cover your mistakes. Pray daily that your gracious Father will allow your children to remember the good experiences and the times when you loved them well instead of remembering the less-than-perfect times.

What's Next?

Commit to praying, and then plan...again and again. Proverbs 16:3 (NLT) says, "Commit your actions to the Lord, and your plans will succeed." Dream with God about what it looks like to love your children well. This summer is a perfect opportunity to improve! In your prayer time, ask God for His schedule, His activities, His divine plan. Then make your plans accordingly.

journal

_____
_____
_____
_____
_____
_____
_____
_____
_____
_____
_____
_____
_____
_____
_____
_____
_____
_____
_____
_____
_____
_____
_____
_____
_____

for
the

The steamy Texas Gulf Coast summer has us searching for recipes that are cool and refreshing. When the merciful Southeast wind blows some of the heaviness from the air, we head outside to grill, sparing our precious, air-conditioned house from the heat of the oven. This family-favorite side dish compliments any meat we serve. It is so well-liked, the kids (and their parents) hover around the bowl with chips in hand to devour it's yumminess before it gets to the plate to accompany our meal! Children can help prepare this simple dish. Be sure to make enough for the appetizer, too!

AVOCADO & FETA SALSA   By: Melissa Lain

Ingredients

2 avocados

4 chopped Roma tomatoes

½ cup chopped red onion

1 bunch cilantro, chopped

4 oz feta crumbled

2 tablespoons olive oil

1 tablespoon red wine vinegar

1 tablespoon cumin

1 teaspoon Kosher salt

Cracked pepper to taste

½ lime, juiced

Directions:

1. Wash and dry the skins of the avocados. Cut lengthwise down the center, pop out the seed. Use a table knife to slice avocado meat up, down and diagonal within the skin. When the meat of avocado is diced within the skin, use a spoon and scoop the meat in a large bowl. Repeat on remaining avocado.

2. Add remaining ingredients to bowl and mix gently.

3. Chill and serve with tortilla chips, crostini or pita wedges.

Summer of Joy

~ Week Nine ~

"I have seen what is best for people here on earth. They should eat and drink and enjoy their work because the life God has given them on earth is short."
 – Ecclesiastes 5:18-20

Hello, Help Club Mamas!

Can you believe it's August already? I can't!

As the school year is quickly approaching, I find myself feeling discouraged as I look back over my summer and realize it was not all I thought it would be. Back in May, I imagined lazy days at home, reading with my children, swimming, trips, playdates, and lots of family time.

It's not that those things didn't happen; they did! But so did lots of whining, complaining, tempers flaring (both the kids and mine), and the feeling that bedtime couldn't come fast enough. With four kids ages seven and under, my life almost never plays out how I intend.

The good news is that God has been so gracious and given me the gentle encouragement I need, so I can give myself grace and finish out this season well.

Maybe you are in my same boat and needed to hear this today!

I love this quote by Zig Ziglar: "Where you start is not as important as where you finish!"

Praying for you and me this week to end this season WELL and for a renewed and refreshed mind to serve our children and families with a heart like Jesus!

With love,

Krystle Porter and the Help Club For Moms Team

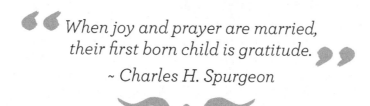

When joy and prayer are married, their first born child is gratitude.
~ *Charles H. Spurgeon*

Mom Tips

By: Leslie Leonard

The wise woman builds her house.
~ Proverbs 14:1a

The Wise Woman Builds Her Spirit

Write 1 John 4:17-19 in your journal. Answer the following question in your journal: How do you show love to your family, your neighbors, and perfect strangers?

The Wise Woman Loves Her Husband

Pray for your husband every day this week during your quiet time. Pray that your marriage will grow and be strengthened, that he will grow closer to your children, and that he will be the light of Jesus while he is away from the home.

The Wise Woman Loves Her Children

Teach your children Psalm 98:1 this week. Take an afternoon and sing praise-and-worship songs together. In our home, we often sing "Jesus Loves Me" for a nighttime lullaby.

The Wise Woman Cares For Her Home

As summer begins to wind down and the beginning of the school year is on the horizon, stock up on your children's back-to-school supplies now. If you start early, you should be able to find the correct items in the requested colors without making multiple trips to multiple stores. Now may also be a good time to work on setting the household budget. Start small if needed by setting a grocery budget. Do your best to stay within your set budget this week. This habit of being a good steward will begin to flow into the rest of your home.

"Many are the plans in the mind of man,
but it is the purpose of the Lord that will stand."

~ Proverbs 19:21 (ESV)

Great Expectations

By: Julie Maegdlin

How has your summer been? Is it going the way you thought it would? At the start of every summer, I always had great plans for what we would accomplish. We would start our days with glorious hikes in the mountains. We would plant a garden in the backyard and make all of our meals from its abundance. Lazy afternoons would be spent journaling and dreaming. And we would almost always finish the nights with gazing up at the starry sky and contemplating the wonders of God.

That is not exactly what it looked like in reality. Instead, we had a constant stream of dirty dishes, dirty laundry, and dirty faces. Kids ran in and out of our house making the thought of a schedule almost impossible, and I was good if I could get to Costco to buy enough food for whoever ended up at the dinner table that night. We did have lots of late nights under the stars, but only because we would eat so late that I was still cleaning the kitchen and straightening the house from the day's activities. However, our reality ended up being as perfect as the dream.

I had to let go of my great expectations for what a summer should look like and embrace what it did look like. I relaxed into what my family thought was a great idea for the day instead of insisting on my own well-thought-out plans. And we had a ball. We did get some hikes in, although sometimes they were more like walks around the park by our house. We did eat well, although sometimes we had macaroni and cheese and frozen peas. We spent countless nights lying on the trampoline, just being together. I am sure we were all contemplating the mysteries of God in our ways in our own minds.

Go Deeper:

Dear moms, let go of what you think it should look like and embrace what it is. Enjoy the gift of the day and relax into it. When we invite God into each day, He can make it holy. The wonder of watching ants on the sidewalk in front of your house can be every bit as exhilarating as the view from a mountaintop. You can still contemplate the wonders of God from your kitchen sink. And a trip to the local ice cream store can be just as tasty and fun as picking a fresh strawberry from your garden.

What's Next?

Stop and look around. If it doesn't look like what you thought it would, is it still good? Are you following the Lord, loving Him with all of your mind, soul, spirit, and strength? Are you sharing that love with your children and their friends? Make your focus about loving God and loving your neighbors and let the rest go. Ask God to show you how to love like He loves. Listen to your children when they express delight over something. Relax into the plans that God has for your summer. After all, He is the creator of mountaintops and ladybugs. He is the One who placed those stars in the night sky. He gave someone the idea of ice cream and strawberries. He created you and placed your children in your home. He can bless each day with His abundance and joy.

"You shall love the Lord your God with all your heart...and with all your mind." – Matthew 22:37 (ESV)

Journal

"They seldom reflect on the days of their life,
because God keeps them occupied with gladness of heart."
~ Ecclesiastes 5:20

"There is a time for everything, and a season
for every activity under the heavens..."
~ Ecclesiastes 3:1

Bloom Where You're Planted

By: Deb Weakly

"In this world, you will have trouble. But take heart! I have overcome the world." – Jesus Christ (John 16:33)

When I read these words of our Lord Jesus, part of me feels comforted, and part of me feels concerned. The truth is, we do experience trouble and heartache on this earth. So how can we live a life of faith when we experience the trouble Jesus speaks about without becoming bitter and discontent when the hard times come?

I have prayed a lot about this over the years, and I feel the Lord wants to teach us to live in our season, or simply, bloom where we're planted. Here's a little object lesson the Lord used to teach our family how to bloom where we're planted. My husband, Randy, grew up in the country and deeply desired a house for us on a little piece of land. In Colorado, the land is very expensive, so we had to wait many years.

Eventually, our miracle did come. We listed our home, it sold in two weeks, and we quickly had a contract on another house with land. Meanwhile, we had to move into a rental for a short time while we were in between homes. The only way this plan would work financially was for us to sell some investments we had saved for 11 years in hopes of one day buying a home.

All of this happened in September 2008, days before the big stock-market crash. To make matters worse, my husband and I were so busy scrambling to find a rental that we forgot to sell the stock, and you guessed it, we lost the majority of our money in the crash! We were devastated and moved into the rental having to pay several thousand dollars to back out of the contract for the home with land we could no longer afford.

But you know what? The Lord works in mysterious ways, and we ended up experiencing a season of great joy in that rental. Most of our boxes were still packed, but we hosted parties, read lots of books together, had a great Christmas, and enjoyed a simpler life. Randy and I still reflect on that time and wonder how on earth we got through it without feeling completely disappointed.

I think God filled up our hearts with the joy that didn't come from our circumstances. When the difficulties began, we started praying Ecclesiastes 5:20 together in our prayer time: "They seldom reflect on the days of their life, because God keeps them occupied with gladness of heart." This is what God did; He kept us occupied with gladness of heart.

Difficult circumstances are going to arise in your life, and I would encourage you to ask God to help you see what He wants to bring into your life at that moment. In the words of Paul, the secret of being content in any and all circumstances is this: "I can do *all* things through Him who gives me strength" (Philippians 4:13).

During challenging times, ask God to strengthen you and to help you bloom where you're planted. Make the most out of your life no matter where you find yourself. Open your hands to the Lord and release everything to Him. God can be trusted. Take His yoke upon you and learn from Him so you can be ready for your calling that is to come.

Go Deeper:

As you think about today's study, pray and ask God to reveal any areas of your life that you can't seem to release to Him. Write them in your journal. Ask God to help you be content in His love and live your life to the fullest in every season with the help of the Holy Spirit.

What's Next?

How can you bloom where you're planted in your particular circumstances? Write down three things you can do this week to make the most out of your situation. Be a good example for your children and involve them in the process!

A Note from Deb: Many months after we moved into our rental, a wonderful home went to auction, and we were able to purchase it! This house was better than the one we were going to build, and it was much cheaper. We get to use our house all the time for events as well as hosting year-long interns from a local ministry. God's plan worked out so much better than ours!

journal

_____
_____
_____
_____
_____
_____
_____
_____
_____
_____
_____
_____
_____
_____

"Peter turned and saw that the disciple whom Jesus loved was following them. (This was the one who had leaned back against Jesus at the supper and had said, 'Lord, who is going to betray you?') When Peter saw him, he asked, 'Lord, what about him?' Jesus answered, 'If I want him to remain alive until I return, what is that to you? You must follow me.'"

~ John 21:20-22

Comparison: The Thief of Your True Identity

By: Samantha Mast

How many times have you looked at someone else's life and compared it to your own? I mean, to be honest, I do this all the time. I am sure at least one mama out there can relate to me.

I have seen someone with a cute outfit and thought, "Wow, I wish I had her outfit." I have been in other people's homes and then thought that my home was ugly in comparison, but the worst area of comparison for me was beauty and body image. I struggled with this for years. I had a hard time believing I was pretty or thin enough and would constantly compare myself to other women. Only when I fully surrendered this battle to Christ was I able to be free from comparison. I accepted myself through Christ's eyes, stopped listening to the world, and believed who God says I am.

There is so much in this life that the enemy will use to distract you. Comparison, if you give in to it, is one of those distractions. When comparing, you are ultimately not trusting God for who He has made you to be.

In the book of John, Simon Peter compared himself to the disciple Jesus loved. In chapter 21 verse 21, Peter wanted to know about John and what the Lord had in store for John's life, just after Jesus had prophesied to Peter about his death. Jesus' response to Peter is great: "If I will that he remain till I come, what is that to you? You follow me" (John 21:22 NKJV).

How often can we relate to the disciple Peter, comparing our lives to others? Here, Peter is more concerned with the disciple John's calling than his own. My natural tendency would be like Peter's, not listening to what God just spoke over my life and instead being concerned with my friend's life.

Surely there is no condemnation in comparison, but Jesus wants us to live in His fullness. His fullness is a life free from comparison. God knows our struggles, and His grace is sufficient for us every day. This awesome Scripture reminds us to follow Jesus instead of being concerned with what other people are doing in relation to us.

Thank God every day for what you have and who you are in Him. Surround yourself with women who will speak truth and life to you. Most importantly, spend time with Jesus in the Word and in worship because this battle starts in your mind.

Romans 12:2 reminds us that we need to renew our minds so that we don't conform to the world. We renew our minds by spending alone time with Jesus.

My prayer is that you would know God made you perfectly; you lack nothing. Spend time with Jesus, and ask Him to remind you of your identity in Him.

As you devote more time to God, you will be less distracted by the world and more content with who you are. Comparison has no control over your life; speak that every day if you need to. Set your eyes on Jesus alone and taste and see His goodness.

Go Deeper:

Do you struggle with comparison? Spending quality time with Jesus every day will make a huge difference in your thoughts and actions.

It is important for you to know who you are in Christ, your identity. Ask the Lord to show this to you.

Do you often look at what others have, what they look like, and how they act, and question yourself in these areas?

What's Next?

Take time for yourself; get alone with Jesus and ask Him to remind you of your identity. If this is new for you, just pray and ask Him to reveal this to you for the first time.

Some things to ask God: What have you designed me to accomplish? What are my purpose and my calling?

Be real, raw, and honest with Him. He knows your heart and your struggles, and wants you to draw near to Him. James 4:8 (ESV) says, "Draw near to God, and he will draw near to you. Cleanse your hands, you sinners, and purify your hearts, you double-minded."

"There is but one good; that is God. Everything else is good when it looks to Him and bad when it turns from Him." – C. S. Lewis, *The Great Divorce*

journal

_____

_____

_____

_____

_____

_____

_____

_____

_____

"Therefore I tell you, whatever you ask for in prayer, believe that you have received it, and it will be yours."

~ Mark 11:24

Pursuing Our Children Like God Pursues Us

By: Tara Fox

Recently, I was on a walk with my children when God laid on my heart that I need to pursue my children as He pursues me. We all have an innate need to be pursued by those who love us; our children are no exception to this need. The beginning of the Bible through the end leads us through the ultimate story of His unfailing love, and we see that God our Father is the pursuer of our souls.

God has designed us as parents to be the first and most important people to model this love relationship for our children. Let's look at how our Father so masterfully does this so we can model our parenting after Him!

1. **He pursues us first (1 John 4:19).**
   We are able to love God because He loved us first. Be the initiator in your relationship! Start your day together by showing your children your love early in the morning. When they are distant, ask the Holy Spirit to show you their immediate needs. Touch is a great way to initiate: giving high fives and hugs, doing hair, and giving back rubs!

2. **He pursues us with kindness (Jeremiah 31:3).**
   It is so lovely how the Lord draws us into relationship with Him by showing us unfailing kindness. Being kind to our child isn't always easy, but it is the way to draw them near. You can use gentle words during heated moments, praise them, write love notes, or just smile!

3. **He pursues us when we are lost (Luke 15:4-6).**
   A child's heart will wander from the safety of close relationship at times. In the Bible, Jesus models this by dropping everything and going after the lost one. When the time comes, we have to clear our schedules and intently focus on keeping our children from possible danger and winning them back for the Lord.

4. **He pursued us to lay down His life (Matthew 20:25-26, 28).**
   So much of our day consists of laying down our lives for our children. Ask God how you can serve your children. Help them with chores, make intentional alone time, invite a friend over, or serve a favorite meal or cup of tea!

5. **He pursues us when we have a bad attitude like Moses, disobey Him like Jonah, mistreat Him like Paul, or even deny him like Peter.**
   This is the hard one for me! Sometimes we need a little break from our children before we pull up our sleeves to do the laborious work of loving them when they are difficult. Often, our children are unloving when they need us most. Spend time with God first, and then take your child out for some one-on-one time. This investment will fill your child's cup and help him or her be tender toward you. A little alone time makes a big difference!

6. His pursuit is ongoing and unending (Psalm 139:7-10).

Our Father never stops going after us! Be encouraged my friend: you are on assignment from the Lord! May seeking their hearts be our life's work. God will give you the energy you need for the long haul to continue seeking your children.

One path to a close relationship with your children is to ask questions and remain attentive when they talk to you. Listening intently to them is the key to cultivating an open relationship through their teenage years and into adulthood. Make sure to look your children in the eyes when they have something to say.

Week Nine

Go Deeper:

Pray with me: *"Father, we need your help to capture our children's hearts–to lay down our lives so that they may feel your uncompromising love through us. Help us not only to seek our children out when it is easy but also when it is hard. May each of your children know that they are worth our pursuit."*

What's Next?

Make a pursuit plan! Ask the Lord where to begin with each child. How can you pursue each of them with touch, conversations, alone time, fun activities, and gifts? Write it down and take the next few weeks or months to spend intentional time with each of your children. Let the Holy Spirit guide you and have fun!

Scripture References

1 John 4:19 "We love because He first loved us."

Jeremiah 31:3 "The Lord appeared to us in the past, saying: 'I have loved you with an everlasting love; I have drawn you with unfailing kindness.'"

Luke 15:4-6 "Suppose one of you has a hundred sheep and loses one of them. Doesn't he leave the ninety-nine in the open country and go after the lost sheep until he finds it? And when he finds it, he joyfully puts it on his shoulders and goes home. Then he calls his friends and neighbors together and says, 'Rejoice with me; I have found my lost sheep.'"

Matthew 20:25-26, 28 "Jesus called them together and said, 'You know that the rulers of the Gentiles lord it over them, and their high officials exercise authority over them. Not so with you. Instead, whoever wants to become great among you must be your servant, just as the Son of Man did not come to be served, but to serve, and to give his life as a ransom for many.'"

Psalm 139:7-10 "Where can I go from your Spirit? Where can I flee from your presence? If I go up to the heavens, you are there; if I make my bed in the depths, you are there. If I rise on the wings of the dawn, if I settle on the far side of the sea, even there your hand will guide me, your right hand will hold me fast."

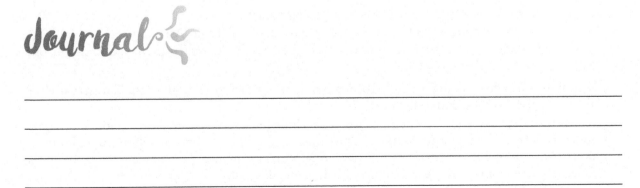

journal

_____

_____

_____

_____

5 Ways to a Better Day with Your Kids

By: Tara Davis

"Love is patient, love is kind." – 1 Corinthians 3:4

I was recently reminded by a mom, more experienced and wiser than myself, that when my children feel filled inside with my love, they are more inclined to obey me and are better able to internalize the lessons I attempt to teach them about the Lord. How true this is! In fact, when I take the time to cover my children with my love, our days go so much smoother than those in which I am rushed and impatient.

Proverbs 22:6 instructs us to "train up a child in the way he should go, and when he is old he will not turn from it." This wise and wonderful mama reminded me that we are called to disciple our sweet children, as Jesus discipled his closest friends, by positively teaching them to identify good and turn away from wrong, and showing them how to live out the love of Christ. We can lead our children by example as we show them love in a meaningful way!

I was encouraged to think of five ways I could fill each of my children's hearts on a daily basis and have shared a few below. Would you join me in discovering effective ways in which you can uniquely fill your child's need for love? I promise you will see a difference in your days with your children as I have seen in mine!

Here are my Five Ways to Fill My Child's Heart Today:

1. Look into his eyes and tell him one thing I appreciate about him.

2. Connect by spending at least fifteen minutes together each day doing something he enjoys.

3. Pray out loud with him and for him.

4. Stop what I am doing and look at him while he is talking to me.

5. Engage with him a few minutes before bedtime by snuggling and talking about his day.

What are your five ways to fill each of your children's hearts this week?

Help Club For Moms is a group of real moms who seek to grow closer to God, closer to our families, and closer to each other. We believe prayer changes everything and God is big enough to help us raise the children with whom God has blessed us.

We focus on digging into God's Word, praying together, and encouraging one another! Through weekly "Mom Tips" and daily "Faith Filled Ideas," the Help Club for Moms helps women take what they are learning about the Lord and apply it to their daily journey as wives and mothers. Our goal is to spread the love of Jesus, inspire women to be the wives and mothers God created us to be and to impact eternity—One mama at a time!

Would you like to be a part of the movement?

Here's how you can get involved in the Help Club for Moms:

- Purchase our books on Amazon. We use 100% of the proceeds to fund our all-volunteer ministry. The titles are: *The Wise Woman Builds, The Wise Woman Cares, The Wise Woman Knows, The Wise Woman Loves, The Wise Woman Stays, The Wise Woman Abides, The Wise Woman Grows, The Wise Woman Enjoys,* and *The Joy Challenge for Moms.*

- Pray for the ministry and the moms in our Help Club Community worldwide—for them to know the love of Jesus and create a Christ-Like atmosphere in their homes.

- Start a Help Club for Moms group at your local church or home. We can help you!

- We are always on the lookout for Titus 2 women who can help mentor our moms through social media and prayer.

- If you are an author, blogger, graphics artist, or social media guru, we need you and your talents at the Help Club!

- We are a 501(c)(3) and all volunteer ministry! Please go to www.HelpClubForMoms.com to help us get God's Word into the hands of moms worldwide!

Questions? Email us at info@helpclubformoms.com.
You can find out more about Help Club for Moms at www.HelpClubForMoms.com and on Facebook and Instagram @HelpClubForMoms.

Church Resource Section

Moms encouraging moms to know the love of Christ

Dear Mom,

We are so very honored that you are journeying through this Bible study with us. What a gift you are to our ministry!

We wanted to make sure you knew that, built right into this book, is everything you need to start a "Help Club for Moms" group of your own! You can do it through your church or even as a small group in your home. Lives are changed when we read God's Word together and focus on becoming intentional moms and wives in community together! Doing a Help Club for Moms Bible Study is a chance for you and your friends to dive deeper into learning about God's design for motherhood. Plus, everything is more fun with friends!

It is so easy to lead a Help Club for Moms group. Each mom commits to following along in the Bible study. Then you meet at your home or church just twice per month to go over what you are learning and pray for one another. We even have a special group on Facebook dedicated to our Help Club for Moms Bible Study Leaders where we give you ideas with lesson plans for your group. Simply go to the Help Club for Moms National Leaders Group, answer the questions and ask to join. It's that simple!

Doing life together as moms in a Christ-centered community draws us closer to Jesus and to each other while building friendship and connections that are sure to last a lifetime. What a great way to walk as moms, together arm-in-arm and with our eyes on Jesus, all the way until we get to heaven.

If you are interested in starting a Help Club for Moms group, either in your church or home, please email us at info@helpclubformoms.com. We would love to walk alongside you, give you helpful resources, and PRAY for you.

Blessings to you, mama!

Sincerely,

The Help Club for Moms Team

FAQ:
About Help Club For Moms

WHAT IS THE HELP CLUB FOR MOMS?

• Help Club for Moms is a community of moms encouraging moms to know the love of Christ. We value authentic, transparent relationships. Together, we study God's Word, pray, fellowship twice a month, and share practical "Mom Tips." All this to become the women, wives, and mothers God created us to be, and with the help of the Holy Spirit, bring up our children to do the same!

WHY CHOOSE HELP CLUB?

• Help Club For Moms offers a Christ-centered program focused on strengthening the church by strengthening moms, through teaching God's design for families and biblically based parenting.

• There is no fee for the program; the only cost is for the books which may be purchased on Amazon.

• The program is for moms of all ages. We love learning from each other in every stage of life!

• There are three simple, but deep, biblical studies per week, which teach and encourage moms, yet are still easy to accomplish. A must for today's busy mom!

• Help Club For Moms "Mom Tips" set us apart from other mom groups because every week, we offer eight practical, new ideas to strengthen and train women in their role as a wife, mother, and woman of God.

• Each mom in Help Club For Moms is partnered with another mom for prayer. Every week, these two moms pray for 10-15 minutes with one another over the phone, deepening their connection with God and each other. Prayer changes everything!

• Help Club For Moms brings godly community, support, fellowship, and friendship to families through the relationships formed between moms.

• HCFM's has three years of Christ-Centered curriculum.

• HCFM has a strong presence on social media, which helps moms go deeper in the studies with other moms around the world.

WHAT ARE THE CORE VALUES OF HELP CLUB FOR MOMS?

• HCFM values authentic and transparent community between moms, deep growth in relationship with God, intentional Bible study, faithful prayer relationships between moms, and practical day-to-day ideas and tips for moms.

WHAT IS REQUIRED OF THE CHURCH?

• HCFM's partner churches should plan to help in two ways:
  1. Offer a meeting space for two hours/twice monthly
  2. Help with childcare for two hours/twice monthly

Hosting a HCFM's Meeting

WHAT DOES A TYPICAL HELP CLUB FOR MOMS MEETING LOOK LIKE?

• Hosting a Help Club meeting is easy and fun and is a great way to build community with the moms in your church or neighborhood. Below is a sample morning meeting schedule. (You could also host a "Help Club Mom's Night Out Potluck Dinner" instead of a daytime meeting for working moms or moms who want some time away while dad has the children.)

SCHEDULE

9:30-9:40   **Welcome, pray, and on time drawing with an inexpensive prize**

9:40-10:15   **Moms meet in groups to discuss current HCFM Bible study**
- Large groups: Moms sit around tables in small groups of 3-6 moms with a leader and possible co-leader to discuss content from the last two week's topic.
- Small groups or home study group: Moms sit in a circle as one big group to discuss content from the last two week's topic.

10:15-10:30   **Simple worship and announcements** (HCFM Spotify and Amazon Prime playlist and lyrics provided if desired)

10:30-10:35   **Book Review** (HCFM suggested book review provided if desired)

10:35-10:50   **Mom Tips in Action** (Invite one of your leaders/ helpers to spotlight a Mom Tip from this week's study and how she used it) Then, invite other moms from the group to share how they used a moms tip from the list or how they are planning to use one in the future. This is an important time for our moms to learn from each other.

10:50-11:15   **Devotion time**
There are two ways to facilitate a HCFM's devotion portion of the group: one led by a seasoned mom or one led by a young, peer aged mom.
- Both groups lead a discussion about the topic from the last two weeks of study by discussing Scripture and asking questions of the group about the topic. (Scripture applicable to the topic and "Questions to Ponder" are found in each study.) The leader shares her personal experiences as a fellow mom journeying on the road of motherhood. The leader may also choose to watch a portion of a Help Club for Moms "Mentoring Monday" video about the topic with the moms in her group.

11:15-11:25   **Moms pray with prayer partners**

11:25   **Pray and dismiss moms to pick up children**

All HCFM leaders have access to a private Facebook group (Help Club for Moms National Group Leaders) where they can access training videos, ask questions, and share ideas to help them host a successful group. **Questions? Email us at info@helpclubformoms.com.**

Book Recommendations

BOOKS FOR MOMS (NON-FICTION):

Parenting the Wholehearted Child
  by Jeannie Cunnion

You and Me Forever by Francis and Lisa Chan
  (marriage)

Daring Greatly by Brene Brown

The Ragamuffin Gospel by Brennan Manning

Love and Respect by Dr. Emmerson Eggerichs

Love and Respect in the family
  by Dr. Emmerson Eggerichs

Mother and Son by Dr. Emmerson Eggerichs

The Circle Maker by Mark Batterson

The Power of a Praying Wife
  by Stormie O' Martian

The Power of a Praying Parent
  by Stormie O' Martian

The Read-Aloud Family by Sarah Mackenzie

BOOKS FOR MOMS (FICTION):

Mark of the Lion trilogy by Francine Rivers

Redeeming Love by Francine Rivers

Sarah's Key by Tatiana de Rosnay

The Help by Kathryn Stockett

BOOKS FOR KIDS:

Discipleship books:

The Picture Bible published by David C. Cook

The Jesus Storybook Bible by Sally Lloyd-Jones

The Action Bible by Sergio Cariello

Missionary Stories with the Millers
  by Mildred A. Martin

Upper Elementary/Early Middle School (grades 4-7):

The Wingfeather Saga by Andrew Peterson

The Green Ember series by E.D. Smith

The Penderwicks series by Jeanne Birdsall

Lower Elementary (grades 2-3):

The Imagination Station by Marianne Hering

Greetings from Somewhere by Harper Paris

Dear Molly, Dear Olive by Megan Atwood

Early Readers (grades K-1):

Owl Diaries by Rebecca Elliot

I Can Read! Princess Parables by Jeanna Young

Jotham's Journey series

Little House on the Prairie by Laura Ingalls Wilder

The BFG by Roald Dahl

The Lion, The Witch, and the Wardrobe
  by C.S. Lewis

Anne of Green Gables by Lucy Maud Montgomery

HOMESCHOOLING:

Teaching From Rest by Sarah Mackenzie

Educating the WholeHearted Child
  by Clay Clarkson with Sally Clarkson

Seasons of a Mother's Heart by Sally Clarkson

Podcasts

PODCASTS FOR MOMS:

Don't Mom Alone

Coffee & Crumbs

Java with Juli

Cultivating the Lovely

Parenting Great Kids with Dr. Meg Meeker

Focus on the Family

The Messenger Podcast

Conversations with John and Lisa Bevere

I am Adamant Podcast by Lisa Bevere

Read Aloud Revival

Happy Hour with Jamie Ivey

PODCASTS FOR KIDS:

Stories Podcast

Storynory

Brains On! Science Podcast for Kids

Adventures in Odyssey

ONLINE SERMONS:

ChurchoftheHighlands.org

Theaterchurch.org

Worship Music

PANDORA HELP CLUB FOR MOMS STATION:

https://pdora.co/2KynyvV

SPOTIFY HELP CLUB FOR MOMS STATION:

https://spoti.fi/2lVBMbw

Plan Sheets

Daily Plan

Date:_____

M T W T F S S

Weekly Memory Verse:

"

"

3 Things I am Grateful for Today:

1.

2.

3.

Notes:

6 Most Important List:

1.

2.

3.

4.

5.

6.

Meal Planning:

Breakfast:

Lunch:

Dinner:

Cleaning:

O 15-min. area _____

O 5'o clock pick-up

Weekly Plan

	Sunday	Monday	Tuesday	Wednesday	Thursday	Friday	Saturday
6:00							
7:00							
8:00							
9:00							
10:00							
11:00							
12:00							
1:00							
2:00							
3:00							
4:00							
5:00							
6:00							
7:00							
8:00							
9:00							
10:00							

Daily Plan

Date:_____

M T W T F S S

Weekly Memory Verse:

"   "

3 Things I am Grateful for Today:

1.

2.

3.

Notes:

6 Most Important List:

1.

2.

3.

4.

5.

6.

Meal Planning:

Breakfast:

Lunch:

Dinner:

Cleaning:

O 15-min. area _____

O 5'0 clock pick-up

Weekly Plan

	Sunday	Monday	Tuesday	Wednesday	Thursday	Friday	Saturday
6:00							
7:00							
8:00							
9:00							
10:00							
11:00							
12:00							
1:00							
2:00							
3:00							
4:00							
5:00							
6:00							
7:00							
8:00							
9:00							
10:00							

44608766R00080

Made in the USA
Middletown, DE
10 May 2019